Sunshine
for the
Latter-day
Saint
Woman's
Soul

Sunshine
for the
Latter-day
Saint
Woman's
Soul

BOOKCRAFT
Salt Lake City, Utah

Library of Congress Catalog Card Number: 99-72529

ISBN 1-57008-652-4

Second Printing, 1999

Printed in the United States of America

Contents

Motherhood

Service and Compassion

Faith and Hope

Marriage and Family

Finding Peace and Balance in Life

Finding Joy and Humor in Life

$\mathscr{P}$reface

Following the pattern of *Sunshine for the Latter-day Saint Soul, Sunshine for the Latter-day Saint Woman's Soul* is packed with 101 stories, poems, and anecdotes to brighten the soul of any mother, wife, visiting teacher, sister, daughter, aunt, or grandmother. This volume of uplifting material focuses on the needs, talents, challenges, accomplishments, and observations unique to women.

Including stories from authors Anita Canfield, Elaine Cannon, Janene Wolsey Baadsgaard, George Durrant, Brookie Peterson, Ardeth G. Kapp, Elaine L. Jack, as well as many others, this collection has a little something for everyone. Stories of faith and hope, poems of gratitude, and anecdotes of love and motherhood will prick your heart and gladden your life. Certain to become a favorite in your home, *Sunshine for the Latter-day Saint Woman's Soul* will brighten your days for years to come.

Bookcraft acknowledges the talents of the many authors who have provided these wonderful stories, and thanks them for allowing them to be included in this collection. The publisher also thanks Lesley Taylor, Carrie Draper, Debbie Redman, and Eden Rasmussen for their help in selecting and compiling the 101 inspiring stories and poems contained in this volume.

Love

The Chosen One

KATHERINE R. WARNER

Many lessons are learned by those who have been through difficult experiences in life. We learn by recreating values through our own behavior. By taking advantage of our opportunities we bring new vitality to our ideals and beliefs.

So it was with Nurse Ann, our middle daughter—angel of mercy—who had helped others in their sick beds with her tender, sensitive care, and who would again make the situation easy. Her motives were pure and her attitude right. There was no hiding it. Her big smile made her upcoming sacrifice acceptable and logical to all. And yet perhaps it was the most difficult for her—married only a year, and moving away from home to Tacoma, where her husband John would begin at law school and where they hoped to begin their family. It was already a disruptive time in her life—a time of change.

The family was gathered waiting for Dad to come and announce the results of the tissue-matching process. Along with our extended family and our ward we had fasted and prayed that one of us would be a perfect match for the kidney that Wid, our youngest son—twenty-three at the time—needed so desperately. Each of Wid's two brothers somehow took for granted that he would be the one, and each had already begun preparing his affairs for the needed three weeks away from work. It was as though each was vying for the privilege to make this sacrifice for his brother.

It was just two months earlier that Wid had called his doctor-father complaining of severe headaches that had plagued him during his final university exams. Dad had taken his blood pressure and found it elevated more than enough to account for the headaches. This had led to a series of tests during the following week. We could hardly believe the results: Wid had kidney failure. He had always been the picture of health, lean and strong, routinely passing the annual physical exams required of him as a college wrestler.

His father decided to contact a colleague in Seattle who had made his medical reputation by starting the first program for long-term kidney dialysis. This friend, Dr. Schribner, suggested we bring Wid for an examination. We left the next day.

Our summer home for several years had been a sailboat we kept on Puget Sound. Living aboard provided us with a glorious way to return to the simple life. Since the boat had no modern conveniences—no TV, phone, refrigerator, or electricity—everything took time. We saw the world in slow motion, and savored a baked potato which took two to three hours to bake in our oil stove. This was Wid's favorite way of life, and it seemed right that we return to it for a restful cruise to try to restore his health.

It was now the middle of June, and the doctor thought Wid had enough kidney function left to keep him from requiring dialysis for a year or so, provided he would maintain a strict salt-free diet. So we loaded our boat with salt-free provisions and set out on a week's cruise with Wid and his expectant wife of a year and a half, Mary Lee, to explore the coast of British Columbia—their favorite vacation spot.

Wid enjoyed the sailing, but that was the extent of it. He did not respond to the diet and felt progressively worse each day, even though each person aboard had dedicated the week to trying to make him comfortable—almost to the point of forcing him to improve. We played games, and we rendezvoused with dear friends who provided diversion and additional support. We read scriptures and discussed their relevance to our lives and Wid's situation—all the time in concentrated communion with our Heavenly Father, pleading for his healing powers to be with Wid. But by the time we returned to Seattle the color of Wid's face had turned ashen grey, and avoiding dialysis was no longer an option.

While Wid underwent those repeated wrenching procedures, each of his siblings and his parents submitted blood samples for matching as the potential kidney donor.

By August we had gathered to hear the results of the tissue typing, which had been flown to Seattle in a special temperature-controlled container. In the meantime each of us had had time to think of the possible consequences and our motives for offering this gift.

One brother said: "I am not worthy. I wanted to do it for the wrong reason—so I could become closer to Wid like his other brother has been all these years."

The other brother said: "I am prepared to give, but to me the glamour of giving a kidney is no big deal. I think it is how we treat each other—our wives, family members, and our fellow-men—on a day-to-day basis that truly matters."

A younger sister felt she was too young for this kind of sacrifice, but willing if she should be the chosen one.

For the parents, the natural thought was, "Let it be me."

Sister Ann and her husband, John, had time to think of how Ann's having only one kidney would affect their plans for having children. Would her health be in jeopardy? How important were their plans for having a family compared to giving a brother new life? She and John had discussed the pros and cons and planned it all out, and when she arrived at our family gathering—the last one to come—we all knew by the serene look on her face when she came through the front door that she knew she would be the chosen one.

"I am the one," she said. "I've known it for a long time. I am happy to be the one!"

Those of us who have seen Wid move around normally for these past eight and a half years, run three to five miles each morning, father four children, fulfill his Church assignments, and realize he is the recipient of the gift of life from his sister, must admit they are witnessing a miracle. But is not each of us a miracle? We, too, have a new lease on life. Our Elder Brother provided this for us.

Although each was willing to give, there was only one who was chosen; only one whose proffered gift would be acceptable. The opportunity to really give and be the only one for a particular job—whether giving a kidney, time for your child, love and support for a family member, or service in a particular calling—that is the key. To be chosen to give, in my opinion, is the most cherished blessing any of us can have. "There has been a day of calling, but the time has come for a day of choosing; and let those be chosen that are worthy. And it shall be manifest unto my servant, by the voice of the Spirit, those that are chosen; and they shall be sanctified." (D&C 105:35–36.)

$\mathcal{I}$n Heaven with You

ELAINE CANNON

There once was a perky three-year-old, wise beyond her years and charming already, too. She's grown now into the lovely lady her beginnings promised. What makes her memorable is something that happened when she was three and living in London with her parents.

Following a big meeting of people who love the Lord, she stood beside a woman who had just given a talk. To the little girl it must have seemed like a long talk, but as the crowd pressed about the woman, a veritable stranger to the child, the little one reached to tug at the lady's skirt. It caught the woman's attention and she looked down into a face, small and radiant, full of innocence and love. The child's eyes held the woman's as she in her small voice said, "I love you. I want to be in heaven with you."

Baptism of a Less-Than-Perfect Family

MARILYNNE TODD LINFORD

In one of the wards we lived in, a family was baptized into the Church. This family was, well, not quite like the rest of the families in the ward. The husband was a blue-collar worker in what would be considered a yuppie ward. The wife had not had much opportunity for education and her grammar and word choices were interesting. They had two daughters, ages eight and ten. The members of the ward were wonderful. They put their arms around this family and made them feel loved. I'll confess I didn't think it would work. I wanted them to look and act like everybody else. I wanted their grammar fixed. I wanted the daughters to wear clothes like the other girls in the ward. I was young and hadn't experienced the way the Lord works.

The mother was called to teach the three-year-olds in Primary. She accepted, but when the Primary president went to her home to give her the manual, she changed her mind and said she couldn't do it. After much encouragement from the Primary president, this woman admitted that the reason she couldn't teach was that she couldn't read. A sister was called to read the lessons to her so she could teach. Little by little she learned to read by having the Sunbeam manual read to her.

This convert sister noticed that many of the young people in the ward could play the piano. She wanted her daughters to play the piano. She traded house cleaning for lessons for her girls. We moved away and I lost track of this family.

About six years later I happened to be reading the *New Era* contest issue and was flabbergasted to see the picture and name of the oldest daughter of this family, who had won first place in the music composition category. A short time later, I received a Christmas card from a friend in that ward. She included an update of who was doing what in the ward. The sister who hadn't been able to read was the Relief Society president!

Another illustration of faulty judgment happened when a man of our acquaintance grew a ponytail. I had noticed this change for several months. One Sunday he walked into a stake meeting as the opening song was being sung. I whispered to my husband, "Does he have some kind of job, like playing in a band or something, where he thinks a ponytail helps?" Richard smiled at me and continued to sing exactly where we were in the hymn: "Who am I to judge another . . . ?" ("Lord, I Would Follow Thee," *Hymns,* no. 220.)

Love Did
What Anger Never Could

SHERRIE JOHNSON

When our children were younger, December was such a hectic, demanding month that by Christmas day I was usually drained both physically and emotionally. In order to "recharge my battery" I would reserve the day after Christmas for myself. On that day the children were involved with friends and new playthings, and we could subsist on Christmas leftovers.

One particular year I had decided that I would spend "my day" reading the Doctrine and Covenants. The morning of the appointed day came and I snuggled into the den couch and began with section 1. I stopped only to feed the family, and by the end of the day I was filled to overflowing with joy and the Spirit. To spend an entire day with the scriptures was a fantastic experience. But at the end of the day I wasn't through with the reading and it was such a wonderful experience that I decided to take part of the next day and finish.

The next morning I picked up where I had ended the day before. It was even more wonderful. My mind seemed to explode with knowledge and my heart pulsed to new heights of joy and love. But two unsupervised days proved to be too much for the children. By the afternoon of that second day they were quarreling and contending. I could hear them in the other room and my heart ached. While I was experiencing a spiritual feast, they were a few feet away fighting! At first I thought they could work it out, but as the screams and shouts got louder I knew I had to intervene. Stalking into the family room, the words, lectures, and accusations that I normally used when upset filled my mind. But when I opened my mouth to speak, the words wouldn't come out. I was amazed! I could feel the words on my tongue, hear them spinning in my head, but I could not utter the awful words.

As I stood there awkwardly, my mouth open, the children stared dumbfoundedly. At that point I did the only thing I could: I fell to my knees, threw my arms around them, and told them how much I loved them. The Spirit communicated with them. Love did what anger never could; the fighting stopped.

A Mother of Seven

DAVID O. McKAY

I am going to tell you the story of a mother who gave birth to no little baby, but who became the loving mother of seven.

Lottie and Burdette had been married seven or eight years and the fact that they had no children was great disappointment to them. Lottie was an only daughter, and had always hoped to have a family.

A second cousin, on her deathbed, asked Lottie to take her baby girl and rear her. This was *Mary*.

A mother in Salt Lake City was left a widow before her second baby was born, and her father told her that if she would find a home for the expected babe, he would set her up in business so she could care for herself and the little daughter she already had. Mrs. Angelina Smith arranged for Lottie to take this baby— *Isabelle*.

> Another little wave
> Upon the sea of life;
> Another soul to save
> Amid its toils and strife.
>
> Two more little feet
> To walk the dusty road;
> To choose where two paths meet,
> The narrow or the broad.
>
> Two more little hands
> To work for good or ill;

Two more little eyes;
Another little will.

Another heart to love,
Receiving love again;
And so the baby came,
A thing of joy and pain.

One evening while Lottie was at a meeting a strange man came to the door and asked Burdette if Lottie Foulger Smith lived here, then handing a large bundle, said, "This is for her," and left hurriedly. Burdette closed the door and the contents of the bundle began to squirm. It was a new-born babe, and Burdette had it in a clothes basket when Lottie returned. The adopted parents named her Eleanor.

Mary had a weak heart from birth, and when she was eleven, she became very ill. Her death was a great sorrow to Lottie, who arranged, through Dr. Rich, to take a fatherless babe from a girl whose family was a respected one. She found solace in this new charge—another baby girl whom they named *Edith*.

One evening when Lottie was out, another bundle was left on a chair on the screened porch. When she returned after dark, she heard the weak cry of a baby only a few hours old—*Alice*.

Later, a father from an adjoining state brought his two motherless daughters (nine and eleven years of age) and asked Lottie if she would be a mother to them, promising to pay for their care. He left, and failed to send a penny for their expense as he had promised. The new parents reared the girls to womanhood—*Virginia* and *Viola*.

The six girls are married and there are several grandchildren. Lottie is a grandmother and as happy as she can be. We pay tribute to her and others who have the willingness and the ability to rear and who possess the divine endowment to love.

$\mathcal{S}$teven Schreyer

BARBARA TIMOTHY BOWEN

We have a friend, Fay Schreyer, whose oldest son was born with a strong body and a handicapped mind. As a teenager, Steven's physical prowess enabled him to enter the Special Olympics as the projected winner in track. He was fast. On the day of the race, he took off like lightning and was many yards ahead of his competitors when suddenly he realized he was alone—his friends were not with him. He stopped, turned around, and, seeing them in the distance, grinned and ran back to greet them and help all of them complete the race together. As he finally came across the finish line, making sure the others crossed to victory before him, a whisper spread through the stunned audience acknowledging that he could have easily won the gold medal. Instead he won whatever is a million steps above gold. We are the ones who are handicapped—at least spiritually and morally. We think life is about finishing the race first. Our children teach us that the winner is the one who finishes the race with the most love and compassion, the one who enjoys the journey and focuses first on helping others get across the finish line.

Rachael

ANITA CANFIELD

My friend Rachael has a wonderful testimony of who she really is. Rachael was born on a ranch in Wyoming to an active Latter-day Saint family. When she was a very young child she became extremely ill and her parents sent for the country doctor. He did all that he could for the small girl, but apparently everyone felt she was dying.

Rachael's father wanted to give his precious daughter a blessing. To prepare himself for this he mounted his horse and rode off onto his ranch among his thousands of sheep. There he prayed as he had never prayed before. He begged the Lord for his daughter's life.

There on his knees, he received the answer. Yes, he could have his daughter's life, if that was his choice. He understood clearly that it was *his* choice, and if he wanted his daughter's life, it would cost him dearly.

There was no hesitation; this loving father told the Lord that Rachael's life was worth any price, even his own life if necessary.

He returned from that prayer, administered the blessing, and commanded his daughter to live. She recovered quickly and was a busy little girl once again.

Within the month, the price for Rachael's life was paid. A huge range fire swept this man's land and destroyed all his thousands of sheep.

As Rachael grew up and learned of this story, she wondered if her life had been spared for a special mission. But when she learned one day the meaning of her name, she no longer wondered: she *knew* she had been spared for a mission. The name *Rachael* means *little lamb.*

Today she is an active, busy, talented wife, mother, and grandmother. She has led a full life, yet there have been no "hall of fame" projects. What, then, was or is Rachael's special mission that she was spared for at so great a price?

For years she wondered if there was something important or significant she had to do. She doesn't wonder anymore; she realizes that her entire life has been her mission. There are important things that Rachael has done; there are lives that she has touched, especially in her own family, that would never have been the same without her. I don't think Rachael is even aware of the most important things she's done.

$\mathcal{L}$ove Among Ashes

ELAINE CANNON

He was like a petite candle now—a white birthday candle—waxen, narrow, unyielding. Death hovered. Surely the struggle soon would be over for them both. He was past caring about being an imposition to others, so mighty was the battle to endure pain and the humiliation of bodily malfunction. She, worn with care-giving in place of her mother who had long since succumbed to an accident, was emotionally depleted as well. She had set her own life aside to be nursemaid to a father who had become a pitiful stranger to her.

She swabbed his mouth, lips, gums, teeth against the ravages of drugs. She used the electric razor lightly, skilled now in man's rightful art. As she brushed his sparse hair she remembered threading her little-girl fingers through luxuriant dark waves. Now there were only memories and wisps and shags of lifeless hair white as the scalp. She recalled the childish delight in smoothing his thick moustache before he laughingly snapped at her fingers. Now thin gruel smeared his upper lip, spills from her spoon-feeding.

She took the damp washcloth and gently wiped his face. Who was this? Where was the man who had been her dear father, so beloved, in fact, that no other man could measure up, qualify as life's companion? She searched for familiarity and comfort among unruly eyebrows too heavy for a forehead taut in death and cheekbones, jaw, and nose unduly protruding—a stranger's face, though she'd cared for it weeks into months.

As the cloth pressed past the sunken eyes they opened and caught hers. There in that instant—communication! It was her father inside that wasted body. The soul of the stranger she had been caring for was indeed familiar to her, and in a wonderful exchange of love their eyes brimmed, the pulse in each quickened, the press of cheek against cheek was real and rewarding. In seconds she knew an incredible gratitude and an outpouring of pure love. Then he was gone.

Life is made of such moments of love which turn proverbial ashes to a harness of hope that one day we'll enjoy that same sociality again, beyond whatever veil separates here and There!

$\mathcal{A}$ Righteous Prayer

BROOKIE PETERSON

The prayers and compassionate feelings of the elderly for others are a welcome blessing. Sometimes our older parents think they are no longer able to contribute to the lives of others, but we can point out that they benefit people in these ways. They can be a truly effective source of help to someone who is discouraged.

The experience that Mary Ann Wood had when she prayed for her husband may be uncommon, but she is an example of an older person who prayed with faith for something which was expedient. Edward J. Wood was the first president of the Alberta Temple, and he served in this position for over thirty years. At one time his voice was seriously impaired; it appeared that he would become speechless.

In her private prayers his wife, Mary Ann, prayed that he would be cured. She asked the Lord to "make me deaf" and restore her husband's voice so that he could do his best in the temple. At that moment the Lord gave her what she had requested. She became deaf and never heard again, while President Wood recovered and could speak powerfully well to the end of his life. This remarkable, faithful sister continued to serve as a worker in the temple for many years.

I Like Pwickely Hair

BARBARA TIMOTHY BOWEN

When I received the phone call that December afternoon saying that my husband had been taken to the University Medical Center after experiencing a grand mal seizure, my heart sank into my stomach and fear filled its place in my chest. I did not want this trial! Quickly, I gathered my three small sons; holding hands, we knelt in a circle and offered a tearful prayer that the Lord would help us, that he'd make things right and put our lives back together the way we had known them. But life was never to be the same again. It was to be harder. It was to be better.

I believe the Lord looks at most of our trials as potential progression, as a means of humbling us so we can become as little children. I don't think he laughs when we look up at him and cry that the ensuing trial is too hard, but he probably smiles like a coach who's just asked us to run the steps of an entire stadium and, putting his hand supportingly on our back, says, "This will be good for you!"

After hours of interminable waiting, the neurosurgeon walked slowly into the room, shook his head, took off his mask, and said solemnly, "It looks much worse than I had expected. I'm sorry." Steve's mother and I stood paralyzed, then stumbled our way down a long corridor until we found sanctuary in a room of exercise equipment; here in this room that symbolizes challenge and hard work, we dropped to our knees and let our tears fall over an old bench press as we pleaded with the Lord to save Steve and to let him raise his children. "Save" is exactly what the Lord had in mind, but not the way we defined it.

When the day finally arrived to bring Steve home from the

hospital, we streamed into his room with balloons and happy faces that tried not to look too surprised at the changed appearance of this man who'd once had a thick head of dark hair. But my three-year-old, his eyes fixed on my husband's head, quickly blurted out, "Where's yo hair?"

"It's gone," my husband replied with a smile.

"Can the docto put back yo hair?"

"No, son."

This little boy paused for a moment, then climbed up on his father's lap, rubbed his hand vigorously across his dad's bristly, stitched scalp, and exclaimed, "Dat's okay. I like pwickely hair!"

Little children have a way of looking at the world with such acceptance that they submit naturally to the will of the Lord. If only we trusted his plan for us this much.

$\mathcal{A}$ Broken Heart

RICHARD M. SIDDOWAY

Pete Walker was the meanest man I'd ever met. Of course I was only twelve years old, but my mother, who was usually quite charitable, didn't think much of Pete either. He lived in one of the older homes in our community. It was built of rock and was set back behind two oversized pine trees. The lawn that survived the neglect of infrequent watering was rarely mowed. Pete moved into the house about five years before my family moved into the neighborhood. My friends warned me to stay away from Pete's house.

In The Church of Jesus Christ of Latter-day Saints, at the age of twelve most young men have the Aaronic Priesthood conferred on them and are ordained to the office of deacon in that priesthood. One of the duties that deacons have is to collect fast offerings. On the first Sunday of each month Latter-day Saints go without food for two meals and contribute at least the cost of those meals to the poor. Deacons are sent throughout the ward to collect these contributions.

After I was ordained a deacon, my first fast Sunday approached. "Who wants district five?" called out Brother Mangus, the financial clerk of the ward. No one volunteered. "Perhaps we ought to give our new deacon that district." He handed me the ten envelopes with an elastic band around them. There was a collective sigh of relief from the rest of the quorum.

I pulled the elastic band from around the envelopes and looked at the name on the first envelope: "Pete Walker." I understood why no one had volunteered for this district.

Although the sun was shining brightly as I slowly crept up his sidewalk, gloom gathered around me. Timidly I stuck my finger forward to ring his doorbell. There was no answer. I heaved a sigh of relief and turned to leave his porch. Suddenly the door behind me was snatched open!

"Whadda ya want?" Pete bellowed. A wave of stale air laced with sweat assaulted my nostrils. "Oh, it's you, kid." He pushed open the screen door and stuck out his filthy hand. I looked into his bloodshot eyes as I handed him the fast-offering envelope. "Wait here," he commanded as he stepped back into his house and shut the door. My heart pounded as I stood on his porch waiting. At length the door flew open and he handed me the envelope. "Now, get outta here!" He brushed the hair out of his eyes with one hand as he waved me away with the other.

I ran down his sidewalk and onto the street. The rest of my fast-offering district was easy. I returned to the ward house and handed the envelopes to Brother Mangus. "Thank you," he said. "This was your first time, wasn't it?" I nodded my head. "Well, I hope you had a good experience." I rolled my eyes and left the clerk's office.

On the Sunday before Christmas I was passing the sacrament—one of the other duties of deacons—and there on the back row sat Pete Walker. He had made an attempt to comb his hair and beard and was wearing fairly clean clothing. I saw him in church the following Easter Sunday. Over dinner my father said, "Looks like Brother Walker's a regular attender. He regularly attends twice a year." He laughed.

For two years I collected fast offerings from Pete Walker. The routine never varied. And I never saw Pete outside his home except at Christmas and Easter. I wondered what he did for a living. No one seemed to know.

When I was fifteen, Martha Louise Draper moved into our ward. The first Sunday she came to church I fell in love with her. I wasn't alone. I think she captured the hearts of every one of the boys in the Aaronic Priesthood. It mattered not to me that she was ten years older than I; she was the girl of my dreams. I learned later in life that commercial advertisers look for girls like

Martha Louise—girls who exude a wholesome beauty—to use in their advertisements. She was blond and pink-cheeked. She smiled freely and displayed even, white teeth. Five minutes after meeting her you felt as if you were old friends. There were only two apartments in our neighborhood. Martha Louise rented the one across the street from Pete Walker.

I found numerous excuses for walking down the street in front of Martha Louise's apartment in hopes that she'd appear. Throughout the summer I continued my excursions. However, I rarely saw her, except at church.

As the summer drew to a close, my friends and I tried to squeeze the last drop of joy from vacation before school began. We rode bicycles ten miles to Lagoon, a local amusement park, and spent our summer wages riding the roller coaster and vainly trying to win prizes on the midway. And then it was over. We glumly boarded the school bus the next morning and rode to school. We grumbled and complained as we checked our schedules for the hundredth time. "Who'd you get for history? Holgren? Forget it!"

The bus ride ended, and I made my way to my first-period class, English. As I walked through the door my perspective on school changed. There stood my teacher, Martha Louise Draper! I thanked whatever fates had arranged my schedule. "Sister Draper," I said, waving at her.

"*Miss* Draper," she replied, smiling. "It's good to see a friendly face. I hope we have a great time this year."

I nodded my head. I now had a reason to come to school. I was certain my attendance would be perfect this year. Class began. Miss Draper led us through the intricacies of Elizabethan sonnets that first term. Never before had I been so captivated by poetry. The end of the term approached.

"I can't believe it!" My mother rolled her eyes as she opened the mail.

My father took the open letter from her hand. It was a wedding invitation. My father's mouth dropped open as he read it. "He's got to be at least fifteen years older than her," he said.

"More like twenty, I'd say," replied my mother.

"Who?" I asked.

"Pete Walker," said my mother. "He's marrying that sweet little Draper girl."

My heart dropped into my shoes. Not my Miss Draper. Not Pete Walker. I picked up the invitation and read it: "Mr. and Mrs. Nolan Draper announce the marriage of their daughter, Martha Louise, to Peter I. Walker, son of the late Mr. and Mrs. Carl Walker. A reception will be held in their honor November 17, from 7:00 until 9:00 P.M., at the home of the bride's parents, 935 East Fountain Avenue. Your presence is the only gift the couple requests."

I thought of how terribly different these two people were. He was so dirty, so unkempt, so uneducated. She was so clean, so pristine, so . . . so . . . so perfect. It was easy to see what he'd seen in her, but what in the world had she seen in him? My heart was crushed.

After dinner I went for a walk. An unseen magnet pulled me toward Martha Louise's apartment. I turned the corner and walked down the street. I looked longingly in her direction. Then, with hate born of jealousy, I looked at Pete Walker's house. The lawn had been cut. The trees had been trimmed. The last remnants of flowers lined the walk. Begrudgingly I thought, *At least he's started taking better care of his house.* I wept as I thought of the two of them living there together.

I went to the wedding reception hoping against hope that the marriage had been called off and Miss Draper was still eligible. She wasn't, but she looked radiant. Pete's hair had been cut, his beard trimmed, and his hands washed. I shook his hand, holding back my jealous anger. Then I grasped Miss Draper's—no, Mrs. Walker's—hand. I tried to summon up courage to kiss the bride, but she thanked me for coming and introduced me to her maid of honor before I could do anything that foolish. I went home, made my way to my bedroom, and wept.

The rest of the school year crept by, and at last vacation began. The first Sunday in June, Mrs. Walker stood in church to bear her testimony. "My dear brothers and sisters, I do so want to thank you for the warm reception I have felt in this ward. Of course it was here I met my dear husband." A gentle murmur drifted through the congregation. I noted with some self-satisfaction that although their house looked much better, Pete still attended church only on Christmas and Easter.

"It has been a hard six years for him. When his mother and father and wife were killed so tragically, he tried to put those memories behind him. That's when he sold his home and moved into this ward. It hasn't been easy for him to work two jobs and go to school. After we married I tried to get him to quit one job. He's too independent. But this next weekend he'll graduate with a master's degree in engineering. He's taken a job with an engineering firm in Arizona, so this will be our last Sunday in this ward. I want to thank you for all of your love and concern for us." She bore her testimony of the truthfulness of the gospel, finished, and sat down. The following week they moved.

My heart healed slowly. The years drifted by. Thirty years passed. My brother-in-law invited us to the baptismal service for my nephew. We travelled the twenty-five miles to their home the following Saturday. We walked into the chapel and sat down. There were six children dressed in white, waiting to be baptized. My brother-in-law and nephew sat on the front row, while the rest of us sat further back in the chapel. I glanced toward a woman sitting across the aisle from me. A vague memory stirred in my mind. The service began. Following an opening hymn and prayer, a short talk was given about baptism. The man who was conducting said, "We're delighted to have six candidates for baptism today. We'd like each of their bishops to come forward and introduce the candidates from their wards. Let's start with the First Ward, Bishop Walker."

A handsome man in his late fifties rose and walked to the stand. He beamed a serene smile as he called my nephew to the stand. After the introduction they walked hand in hand back to the first row, where my nephew sat down next to his father. The bishop continued down the aisle and sat across from me. He smiled at me, and then his brow furrowed. I took a second look at the woman sitting next to him, and realized it was Martha Louise Draper Walker! I looked in amazement at the silver-haired man in the navy blue suit sitting next to her. Bishop Pete Walker!

Following the baptismal service I walked to Bishop Walker and shook his hand. "I used to collect fast offerings from you," I said. A look of recognition swept over his face.

"I'm sorry," he said, "I don't remember your name." His wife stepped to his side and helped.

"Let me introduce you to one of my old students," she said. She completed the introduction. I introduced them both to my wife. "What are you doing now?" Sister Walker asked.

"I'm teaching school," I said. "Computer science and data processing. You inspired me to go into teaching. Obviously you're living here now. The last time I heard you speak, you were going to Arizona."

"You have a good memory. That's been a long time ago. Well, Pete and I lived in Phoenix for nearly five years before we had an opportunity to move back to Utah. We've lived here for nearly twenty-five years. Pete started his own firm about fifteen years ago."

"I'm being really nosy," I said, "but when I used to go collect fast offerings, your husband scared me to death. How in the world did the two of you ever get together?"

She smiled a sweet, serene smile. "One night as I was coming home from school late, I pulled up in front of my apartment and switched off the key in my car. The car kept on running for several seconds. Pete pulled into his driveway about the same time. He came across the street and asked if I needed some help with my car. He was covered with grease and had his bushy beard and hairdo. My first inclination was to run into my apartment and lock the door, but he told me he lived across the street and he'd be happy to adjust my car. I don't know what he did to it, but it ran perfectly.

"I took him a plate of cookies to thank him and we sat on his porch and talked. One thing led to another and we got married."

Bishop Walker said, "This great lady saw right through the dirt, the grease, and the defenses and helped me rebuild my life."

"Would you share your story with us?" I asked.

He nodded his head. "It might take a few minutes. You probably want to visit with your family."

I explained to my brother-in-law that we'd be a few minutes late, and my wife and I made our way to Bishop Walker's office, where we joined the bishop and his wife. We seated ourselves. Bishop Walker rested his chin on his tented hands. "I went on a mission to the Southern States and returned home to a girl who waited for me. We renewed our romance, and about six months later we were married in the Salt Lake Temple. We were driving home to Provo for our reception. I was driving, my new wife was beside me, and my mother and father were in the backseat." His face grew dark as he remembered. "We ran into fog at the Point of the Mountain. I probably wasn't paying as much attention as I should have been. I was probably going too fast. Whatever the case, suddenly I saw brake lights in front of me. I slammed on the brakes and the car skidded sideways into the truck whose brake lights I'd seen."

Tears rolled down his cheeks. "My wife, my father, and my mother were killed. My face slammed into the steering wheel. I broke my jaw, both arms, assorted ribs." He paused for a moment. "I couldn't even attend their funerals; I was in the hospital in traction. We were going to live in my folks' basement apartment. I'm an only child, and when I was finally released from the hospital I returned home to too many memories. The house was mine, but so were the funeral expenses. It took all the money from the sale of the house, plus some more, to pay off all my folks' expenses. My dad didn't believe in life insurance. He thought he was never going to die."

He paused again. "I'm sorry, I'm boring you."

"No, no you're not. Please go on."

"I moved to your ward. I tried to put memories behind me. I thought God had forsaken me. I don't think you can imagine how much guilt I felt. I grew a beard to cover the scars on my face, and I went into seclusion. It didn't take long before I realized I had to go to work, but I really didn't have many skills. I finally got a job at an all-night service station and truck stop. I enrolled at the university and got a part-time job on campus. It took me six years, but I finished my degree. Of course, along the way I ran into Martha Louise."

This time the pause was long enough that I thought Bishop Walker had finished his story. But he cleared his throat and continued: "Do you remember the Lord's statement to Samuel that 'man looketh on the outward appearance, but the Lord looketh on the heart'? Well, Martha Louise went about it the Lord's way. She looked right past the dirty, sweaty, shaggy outward appearance and accepted me as a son of God. There is no doubt in my mind that she saved me from myself." His eyes shone as he looked at his wife. "Gently she brought me back. She loved me into submission. She gave up her great love of teaching her students in order to focus her energy on me. I was frightened to shave my beard. I thought the scars would be too obvious. The scars were more inside than out. It took nearly a year before I started attending church regularly. One day she said, 'Pete, I'm sure the Lord has forgiven you for the accident. Now, when can you forgive yourself?' I realized I'd been blaming God for something I'd done. She is my most treasured companion. She and the Lord together are my salvation." He leaned over and kissed his wife.

My wife and I thanked him and left, hand in hand. "Thank you," I said to her.

"For what?"

"For loving me, with all my imperfections."

She squeezed my hand.

A Woman's Influence

Trudy Is My Neighbor! My Friend!

ELAINE CANNON

The young mother was a real beauty, very chic and trendy, in excellent taste. Her fingernails were salon enhanced. Her shoulder-length hair had been highlighted, and it caught the sun's glow like a halo as beams streamed through the church window. Her knife-pleated skirt flipped enchantingly about her shapely legs, snugly encased in black tights. She finished her Relief Society lesson with a sweet prayer, and the president, Marge, who was not so chic nor so young, stepped quickly to the teacher's side and they embraced, warmly patting each other's shoulder in the tender exchange of love. "Trudy is my neighbor! my friend!" said the president to the women gathered there, before announcing the closing song and prayer. Trudy's eyes filled with tears and her chin quivered as Marge paid tribute to her.

For six weeks in the coldest, snowiest part of the season, Trudy had gathered up her new baby, her toddler, and her eleven-year-old and braved the elements to do kindly deeds for her friend and neighbor, Marge. In disguise as the Relief Society president, Marge actually was the most needful of the sisters. She was a widow. She had undergone back surgery and was having a tough recovery. She lived in a split-level house with steps and stairs she couldn't navigate for a time. All her high-school-age children worked after school to help with the family finances. But Trudy was there to start the washer, fold clothes from the dryer, collect the mail, vacuum, and accomplish some personal grooming for Marge. Others had been assigned to bring in meals, but Trudy brought in heart and hope in such a way that Marge—remembering—counted her as a blessing.

$\mathcal{S}$ister Barnes

BARBARA B. SMITH

There may have been a time when I had no idea what the Relief Society was, but I cannot remember it. From the very beginning of my conscious memory, Relief Society, my mother, and other women are intertwined. The faces of the women were familiar to me and I can still recall many of them clearly—one especially.

In fact, I believe my first introduction to the power of Relief Society is associated with that face; I can recall vividly that it was round, with blue eyes that twinkled. It belonged to a heavy-set woman with a broad English accent—Sister Barnes. She had red hair, and I remember that when she laughed her face crinkled up—at least that's how it looked to me as a little girl.

However, Sister Barnes wasn't always happy. She was from England, and Salt Lake City sometimes seemed a long way from home. At those times she looked sad. I feel certain that my mother, who was then her Relief Society president, knew that Sister Barnes felt lonely, being away from her homeland and the people there who were familiar to her. I believe my mother understood that the strangeness of this new country, even among the Saints, was hard for Sister Barnes.

One day Mother asked Sister Barnes to come to our home to cook her English specialty, fish and chips, for a meeting of the ward Relief Society presidency. They were marvelously delicious and the Relief Society officers asked Sister Barnes if she thought she could cook fish and chips for the bazaar. In those years, before the change in ward budgeting procedures, Relief Societies used to hold bazaars. They were a major event on every ward calendar and the Relief Society's key money-raising effort of the year. The sisters made many items to be sold, including food that always sold very well.

Sister Barnes was obviously pleased when they asked her to cook fish and chips for the bazaar. She said she knew she could do it if she had some women to help her. The presidency assured her that they would supply all the helpers she needed and would furnish the ingredients as well. I don't know how I happened to be in the room at the time that decision was made, but I remember the moment well and remember, too, how happy it made Sister Barnes. I was also at the bazaar, and I recall how Sister Barnes came early and was in the kitchen during the whole evening cooking her delicious fish and chips. Everybody bought some and then came back for more. I think Sister Barnes actually surpassed herself that night, for the fish and chips seemed even better than the first time I'd tasted them.

After that bazaar, Sister Barnes quickly became known in our area. Her fish and chips were in great demand, and so was Sister Barnes. The members of the ward came to value her not only as a capable cook, but as a fun-loving person. Everybody liked her. They just needed to get to know her. The Relief Society and Mother helped bring about that great change. I'm sure Sister Barnes never forgot her native country, but through Relief Society she found new friends and her face acquired a settled happiness.

I thought then, as a young girl, that it was because the fish and chips were so delicious that Mother and her officers had been inspired to ask that capable English woman to make them for the whole ward. Now I know that the inspiration actually came to provide a way of focusing on a wonderful individual and of helping her realize her own worth. Far more important than providing fish and chips for the ward bazaar, the work of Relief Society lay in confirming the gospel teaching that nothing is more important in the heavenly scheme of things than the individual soul.

Becky, a Real MVP

MARILYNNE TODD LINFORD

In the year 1995 the San Francisco 49ers won the Super Bowl, and the Most Valuable Player (MVP) of the series was Steve Young—great-great-grandson of Brigham Young. Steve played for Brigham Young University, and to the children of the Church and of Utah, Steve Young reached hero status. Becky is a third grade schoolteacher about Steve's age. She, like Steve, is single. In Steve's case he is a most eligible bachelor—a fact touted in the press as a plus. In Becky's case, however, she and her family and friends count her singleness as a minus. But Becky does more than just teach. She builds and loves each child who is entrusted to her care for nine months. She works hard to make a difference in each child's life and tries to stay in tune with the feelings and needs of her class. Nearly all the special things Becky does to show love in the classroom day in and day out, year after year, go unnoticed except by an occasional perceptive, thankful parent or child.

Becky sensed excitement building in her class for Steve Young and the San Francisco 49ers as Super Bowl 1995 neared. One day she gathered the children around her and together they wrote Steve a group letter. Many also drew pictures for him. One of the drawings had Brigham Young and Steve Young on pedestals. Another had him going to Disneyland after winning the Super Bowl. One pictured him going to the bank with a sports car full of money. One showed him in front of their elementary school with the caption, "This is the place." These pictures were so good that Becky took twelve of them to the copy shop and had them made into a very cool calendar for Steve (which isn't

cheap!). He responded with a thank-you note written on 49er let-
terhead saying he hoped to meet them someday. Although Becky
didn't dare believe he would really come, she told the principal,
as is her responsibility, that perhaps Steve Young would come to
her class. The principal's reaction was, "Oh, sure."

On *the* day, Steve walked by the principal's office and past all
the secretaries unnoticed. He opened the door to Becky's classroom and asked, "Is this the place?" Becky and the class froze in
a shocked and thrilled moment, grasping the fact that Steve
Young had really come. He autographed every piece of clothing
the students had from socks to hats. He challenged the children
to study hard, follow through with assignments, listen to their
parents, and read, read, read, which he said he does a lot of during football season.

Steve is the central figure in this story. He and his team won
the Super Bowl. He was MVP, has millions in the bank, and still
took an afternoon out of his life to give twenty-seven third
graders and one teacher a lifetime memory—an honest credit to
the kind of person he is. In contrast, the quiet love Becky shows
for her children hasn't made her millions, or given her an MVP
award, or a spot on the evening news; but in the whole spectrum
of people who truly influence others, she's a hero too.

When I observe single women and married-but-childless women
functioning and making a difference in their professions, in their
churches and communities, in their families, I wonder if, in God's
economy, a percentage of childless women is necessary to contribute in a way mothers-of-many can't?

The Highest Place of Honor

DAVID O. McKAY

The true spirit of the Church gives to woman the highest place of honor in human life. To maintain and to merit this high dignity she must possess those virtues which have always demanded and which will ever demand the respect and love of mankind. To know what these virtues are, let everyone think of his own mother. With her picture in mind, each will agree that "a beautiful and chaste woman is the perfect workmanship of God."

Woman possesses power to ennoble or to degrade. It is she who gives life to the babe, who wields gradually and constantly the impress of character to childhood and youth, who inspires manhood to noble ambition or entices and ensnares it to defeat and degradation, who makes home a haven of bliss or a den of discontent, who at her best gives to life its sweetest hopes and choicest blessings.

Anything, therefore, is to be most highly commended and encouraged which has as its motive the ennoblement of womankind—beauty, modesty, sincerity, sympathy, cheerfulness, reverence, and many other sublime virtues must be hers whose subtle and benign influence is such a potent factor in the progress and destiny of the human race.

Words

IDA ISAACSON

Tablets of stone may waste away—
Leaving an image of decay.
A word leaves an imprint on the mind
That may inflame or bless mankind.
An innocent child hears an evil word,
And forever after his memory is stirred.

Words are the stepping stones of thought,
And over a word battles are fought.
The mind selects the intent it will use;
The tongue reveals the mind's hidden views.
So mighty are words they never die;
And time makes no difference to a lie.

To My Visiting Teachers

EMMA LOU THAYNE

I'm glad you came, my friends.
Today was not a day marked on my calendar
in red—or black.
It was just a day.
Until you came.

You came to me
and I was all I had for you to see.
My props and backdrops, even my
    supporting actors
were somehow unimportant on the scene:

Just you. Just me. We three
in good companionship.

Or maybe, yes, I'm sure, there was another
who talked and laughed and felt with us.

Because, here now, behind the door
that I just closed
as you two touched my arm and said
you'd come again

the day is new
and I'm not alone at all.

*L*ife: A Precious Gift

BARBARA B. SMITH

As a child I had been taken to Wyoming to spend some time with my grandmother, who was a country doctor. Once while we were there, she had to make an unexpected house call and took my brother and me along. We had been told to stay in the car as she pulled her black bag from behind the front seat of that big Buick and hurried inside. For a while we sat quietly in Grandmother's car, but soon the children of the household coaxed us to come play with them. We did. Our games took us running around the yard and out by the corrals, and then we burst noisily around one corner of the house. There, framed in the old window, I saw my grandmother washing a newborn infant, and, suddenly, as more children's faces crowded the window to get a peek, my grandmother laughed delightedly. She was laughing because of the safe arrival of the baby she was bathing. She was laughing at the window full of children's faces. And she was laughing because of the joy she felt to be so much a part of the coming forth of a new life. Life is a precious gift. She knew it and I knew she knew it. And now, for myself, I too knew it.

$\mathcal{A}$ Visiting Teacher Is . . .

KATHLEEN "CASEY" NULL

I've had visiting teachers of my own ever since my college days. They've come in all kinds of shapes and sizes and brought me lots of things I needed.

A visiting teacher brings me an oasis of calm in a desert of chaos.

A visiting teacher is a miracle: a friendly adult face in my home in the middle of the day!

A visiting teacher is a friend who brings me a pizza on the day I get my appetite back after a bout with the flu.

A visiting teacher remembers my birthday and forgets which one it is.

A visiting teacher is someone who offers a prayer before she knocks at my door and offers a helping hand before she leaves.

A visiting teacher is someone to laugh with about the things I'd be crying about if she hadn't arrived.

A visiting teacher enriches me with her personal interpretation of a familiar lesson, complete with real-life anecdotes that let me see how human and vulnerable she is, like me.

A visiting teacher can sabotage my diet with one sweet impulse.

A visiting teacher brings me the peace of an all-night sister-to-sister talk in fifteen minutes.

A visiting teacher sees me at my worst and still comes back anyway.

A visiting teacher provides me with potted plants, potpourri, and other feminine whimsies I ordinarily deny myself.

A visiting teacher is very tolerant of chaotic childhood as she sits calmly in the midst of it—in my home.

A visiting teacher shows my observant children that Mom is meant for more than just making peanut butter sandwiches.

A visiting teacher reminds me, with a spiritual break in a busy day, of sisterhood and eternity.

And with my heart full of the gifts brought by my sisters, I return to the peanut butter sandwiches with renewed perspective.

$\mathcal{F}$ar-Reaching Effects

ANITA CANFIELD

I met a woman some years ago. She was single, never married, and a popular teacher at a western college. She watched as her younger sisters grew up, married, and had families. She pondered her own place and purpose in life. She decided early that, yes, she would have a happy, productive, useful life even if she didn't marry. Life had to hold meaning because she believed that the Lord loved her as much as he loved married women, and he needed her, too.

This woman is also a seminary teacher and dearly loved. Students from church and school flock to her home. Day or night you can find young people there, sharing food, thoughts, music, and laughter. Her home is filled with those young hearts she constantly teaches and inspires.

A few years ago she was feeling overwhelmed. She was reaching an age at which it became clear that the hopes and dreams she'd had since her youth would never come to pass in this life. At her age she once expected to have a husband, home, and family. This no longer seemed possible and she was feeling a little sorry for herself.

When she was counseling with her bishop about the possibility of serving another mission, the bishop asked her to reconsider because she was so very much needed there in her community. Before she left his office he asked if he might give her a blessing. In essence she was told through the blessing that hers was a great "calling" to be single. She was told that she would not realize the far-reaching effects of her life on this earth until she crossed the veil, "for prophets have sat in your classes." She was counseled that she could not have been such an effective instrument in the lives of young people if she had had children of her own, but that she would yet be a mother, a "mother of multitudes and multinations."

This good sister has allowed me to share this with you because of her ability to care and to love others. She is one of the choicest women ever to come to earth. The Lord has entrusted her with a great calling and mission. I, too, believe we have no idea, and won't have any idea until we cross the veil, of the influence we have even from day to day.

A Woman's Influence

DAVID O. McKAY

Often a woman shapes the career of husband or brother or son. A man succeeds and reaps the honors of public applause, when in truth a quiet little woman has made it all possible, has by her tact and encouragement held him to his best, has had faith in him when his own faith has languished, has cheered him with the unfailing assurance, "You can, you must, you will."

Helping and loving and guiding,
Urging when that were best,
Holding her fears in hiding
Deep in her quiet breast;
This is the woman who kept him
True to his standards high. . . .

This is the story of ages,
This is the woman's way;
Wiser than seers or sages,
Lifting us day by day;
Facing all things with a courage
Nothing can daunt or dim,
Treading life's path, wherever it leads—
Lined with flowers or choked with weeds,
But ever with him—with him!
Guidon—comrade—golden spur—
The men who win are helped by her!

Motherhood

My Kingdom

SUSAN EVANS McCLOUD

You may close the door upon me,
And think when you are gone,
"Poor thing, she's stuck at home all day,"
How wrong, my dear, how wrong!

I am queen of my own castle,
I hold expectant sway,
For I decree what things will fill
The hours of my day.

There are diapers, true, and dishes,
And work that must be done,
But Mozart keeps me company
And makes it seem like fun.

I can take a walk with baby
Whenever I may please,
And watch the robins peck for worms,
And taste the sweet spring breeze.

Or I may sit by the window,
My Byron on my knee,
And wander strange enchanted dreams
Of worlds that used to be.

I've clothes to mend and tears to dry,
Toys strewn across my floor,
But I have children's laughter, too,
And who could ask for more?

You come home to me, dear, tired
From a world that is cold,
But I have angel lips to kiss,
And golden heads to hold,

And little arms about my neck,
And whispers in my ear.
Your world outside my castle walls
Can't hold such treasures, dear.

I've Decided We Need to Start Seeing Other People

BARBARA TIMOTHY BOWEN

When our middle son, Collin, was in eighth grade, we were arguing over some independence issues one afternoon as I was driving him to a friend's. At this point, my husband had died and I was a single parent, struggling to be both the father and the mother. Finally, I threw up my hands and said, "Collin, I'm frustrated with all the problems in our relationship!" Without a pause, he put his hand kindly on my shoulder and, in a mature voice, said, "Mom, I'm sorry, but I don't think this relationship is going to work. I've decided we need to start seeing other people." I laughed so hard, I couldn't remember why I was ever upset.

*E*xactly How Many
Should We Buy?

EARLENE BLASER

My sister and I had taken a Korean visitor, three of my children, and three of their friends to the Salt Lake Arts Festival. This was a fun place to see various artistic styles and observe artsy people. There were lots of things for the younger children to do and dozens of booths displaying art, jewelry, and clothing for sale. The twelve-year-old (almost thirteen, as she always adds) started begging me to come see this incredible clay jewelry several booths away. I had a pretty good idea the price was unreachable, since this was a fair to which you came to appreciate the artistic skills, not a place to shop for a family of ten. I said, "Sure, let's go see it." Bobbie Jo picked up her favorite piece of black-and-taupe beaded bracelet and, looking up with soft eyes, pleaded, "Can I have this?" "Well, let's see how much it is," I replied. "Seventy-two dollars," the clerks spoke up. I put my arm around Bobbie Jo, leaned in close, and asked, "Exactly how many should we buy?" We all had a good laugh over that. The word no was never mentioned. Needless to say, we did not buy the bracelet or anything else that day. Everyone went home happy and I forgot about the whole thing.

My sister said that as she replayed the scenario in her mind on her drive home, she imagined how she might have handled that situation. She says she would have refused to go look at the bracelet at all because she knew she wouldn't buy it. If she did look, she would have said no before even asking the price, *and* if she knew the price she would have said, "Absolutely not! If I spend $72 on you, then the other three kids would expect me to spend that on them, and that is ridiculous. Do you know how much four times $72 is? You would probably just lose it anyway."

Same results—no bracelet purchased. The first scenario told the child, "Your taste and interests are important to me, and if you desire something, at least inquire about it. You never know—some things are possible." The second example would leave Mom mad that the child was so foolish to have even wanted the bracelet, and the child would confirm that Mom is just a grouch: "She always says no anyway, and she thinks I don't take care of my stuff."

101 Acts That Say "I Love You"

MARILYNNE TODD LINFORD

Listed below is a fraction of the millions of things mothers do, did, or will do for their children. This list highlights things mothers do routinely, often without receiving thanks or praise. Occasionally I remind my children that my actions constitute a major way in which I show love for them—by my works. I prepare a favorite meal to show love; I help with homework to show love; I do the laundry, the cleaning, the disciplining and praying to show love. One mother shows her love by making bread, another by teaching her children to ice skate, another by reading every night to her children, another by working to pay the bills. The intent of the list is to marvel at what mothers do to raise a child or two. Each mother deserves a blue ribbon and a standing ovation. Each of these 101 acts says, "I love you by my works."

Nine months or so before a mother earns that title
She endures morning, or evening, or all-day sickness.
She watches her figure change to give her child room to grow.
She willingly submits to undignified medical tests and exams—
Endures poking and prodding—for the good of her baby.
She feels him kick and rubs her tummy to communicate,
"I'm here; I love you."
She loses sleep and changes her eating habits.
She's concerned, worried, scared,
And physically uncomfortable.
She reads and prepares, plans and shops.
She forgets that there is any other topic of conversation.

On her baby's birth day
She survives the pain of labor and delivery
Or the combined agony and anticipation of adoption.
"Who does he look like?
What will he grow up to be?
Can we raise this precious gift so that he will say,
I was born of goodly parents?"
She nurses or prepares formula and gets spit up on.
She changes diapers approximately five times a day,
For 365 days, for approximately two years—or 3,650 times.
She dresses her baby when floppy head, arms, and legs
Hardly want to go into neck, sleeve, and leg openings.
She walks the floor enduring colicky afternoons and nights.
Mommy and baby take stroller and car rides.
She sings lullabies and they rock together.
She washes miniature clothes and bathes tiny feet and hands.
She prays for her baby and anticipates the first time
She will fold his little arms to help him with his first prayer.
She watches him reach, sit, stand, walk, run, climb,
Learn, set goals, achieve.
All of which she records in her journal
To transfer someday to his baby book.
She gives endless encouragement and praise.
The first few times, she picks him up when he falls,
And then lets him pick himself up.
She tucks him in each night, willingly searching for lost
Blankies and binkies.
When her baby is sick,
She sacrifices a good night's sleep if necessary—
Something she'll do more often
When the dating nights get long.
She tricks the medicine down as in-house doctor and nurse.
She comforts after nightmares and buys night-lights.
Rubbing tiny backs and tying laces in double knots
Become part of her expertise.
She celebrates his birthdays,

Which seem to come way too often.
She prepares three meals a day, times 365 days,
Times about 20 years—or 21,900 meals.
Child-development books become her favorites
To check out at the library.
She learns what to say
When a bad grade shows up on a report card.
She wipes away tears and says,
"You can do it and I will help you."
She teaches study habits and table manners
And she worries about nutrition,
Making sure dinner comes before dessert.
She becomes a certifiable taxi driver and car pool organizer.
She goes to games and recitals
And watches swimming lessons.
She listens to practicing and notes each improvement
Or hint of talent.
She combs, curls, braids, perms, and cuts hair.
She washes and dries smelly gym clothes in record time and
Hopes for the day her children will do their own laundry.
She makes errands in the car fun,
And vacations extraordinarily fun.
She plays the same games and reads the same books—
Over and over.
She conducts pet funerals.
She expresses her love verbally, daily.
She still gives each child room to grow.
She reads scriptures and prays
And teaches the gospel of Jesus Christ.
She helps each child feel good about himself
Celebrating little and big successes.
She likes, or at least endures, her children's friends.
She empathizes with dating frustrations,
Soothing hurt feelings and broken hearts.
She's resident philosopher, psychologist, philanthropist, and
Employer, paying her children for what they should volunteer

To do for free,
All the while teaching the value of money—
How to budget, how to save,
How to make do and do without,
And the blessings of paying tithing.
She exemplifies charity
Helping children think of others' needs first, or at least second.
She teaches organization and goal-setting skills.
She challenges each to do his or her best to reach potential.
She instills work habits, saying,
"If it's worth doing, it's worth doing right."
She has and teaches integrity, saying,
"Right is right even if nobody is doing it, and
Wrong is wrong even if everybody is doing it."
She models a positive attitude.
She hugs and laughs, cries and prays, fears and hopes.
She loves . . .

Love to a mother is more than emotion;
It's action, it's deep, it is total devotion.
It's going and doing, becoming and being
Determined, resilient with infant and teen.

It's deeds never seen, never counted, nor praised;
It's spending a lifetime to get one kid raised.
Thanks, Mom, for the pancakes, for notes on my door,
For years of sack lunches, for socks in my drawer.

I'll try to say thanks, to repay all you've done—
By serving with love generations to come.

Teach Her of Me

SHERRIE JOHNSON

The excruciating pains that periodically seized my body had kept me awake the entire night. I rolled over to look at the clock for the hundredth time. It was six o'clock—finally. Carefully I crawled out of bed. The pains were still only about eight minutes apart, but they had been hard enough to chase away any expectation of sleep.

"I think we'd better call the doctor," I told my husband, Carl.

"Are you sure?" he asked. I'd told him that three times during the previous week only to have the contractions stop shortly afterward.

"They're a lot harder this time."

Carl looked at me. I looked back. Unable to articulate what we were feeling, still we somehow sensed that our love, our relationship, was being reaffirmed and given new potential through this experience of pain and joy.

An hour later we arrived at the doctor's office, a strange mixture of fear and excitement pulsing through me.

By then the contractions were five minutes apart. "Go on over to the hospital and we'll have you a baby before noon," the doctor instructed.

Sensing that my life would never be the same again, I smiled through a pain. All of the days before this moment had been preparing me for all of the days that were to follow. Slowly the hours passed. Noon came and went, and anticipation and joy fought against the pain and fear. By then I wasn't sure this was worth it. Why had I wanted this so much? Why did there need to be such suffering? How could I stand another minute of this?

"Soon, soon!" the nurse kept reassuring. "Just be thankful you're not crossing the prairies in a covered wagon."

"I am. I am," I whispered through clenched teeth as the monstrous pain assaulted me again.

One o'clock slipped slowly by. I was just at the point of complete despair, having decided that the joys of motherhood were much overrated, when everything began to happen at once. At 2:05 P.M. the doctor held up a slimy, red, screaming baby. "It's a girl," he said, as if he'd done it all himself. "Healthy, vocal little girl."

Big tears welled up in my eyes. Joy pulsed through me in electric jolts. I had never seen or experienced anything so beautiful in all my life. "A mother is born," I kept thinking, "and it's me!"

Later, after I was comfortably situated in a room, they brought my daughter to me, washed and smelling like sweet springtime. As I took the warm bundle into my arms, a love unlike anything I had ever experienced surged through me. It didn't seem I could hold her tight enough. How could I possibly express what I was feeling? This was my daughter! I wanted to shout it from the housetops and at the same time savor and protect the secret.

"How will you ever know what I feel at this moment?" I whispered. "How can I let you know how much I love you?"

And then the feeling overcame me, "Teach her of Me."

$\mathscr{S}$leep Well

BARBARA TIMOTHY BOWEN

One October evening, when we'd returned home after seeing *Medicine Man,* my son Adam was determined to sleep outside in a hammock like he'd seen in the movie. I finally consented, but as I was putting on my nightgown, I felt the shivering night air and decided he needed more blankets to keep him from the cold. I grabbed another sleeping bag and headed outside. When I reached the hammock, I stopped. There was Adam with his knees dug in the dirt, kneeling over the hammock, saying his prayers. I was touched and stood silently, pleased, and shaking. It was so cold, I was quite convinced that he wouldn't be long. Three minutes went by, then six, then ten. Then I quit counting. When he finally stood up, I handed him the sleeping bag, and with my quivering voice, more from emotion than from cold, I could only say, "I love you. Sleep well."

$\mathscr{F}$irst Experience

JANENE WOLSEY BAADSGAARD

$\mathbf{M}$ost women's first experience in childbirth could be described as unnerving. I, of course, was too dumb to know I was in labor. When I woke at 3:00 A.M. one night in April, I wasn't alarmed. My baby wasn't due until June. I felt a slight pop and made a quick beeline for the bathroom. My husband and I had spent the entire previous evening guzzling soda pop, and I thought I was paying the consequences for my overindulgence.

"Are you all right, Jan?" I heard my husband whisper drowsily from the bed.

"I think so," I reassured him. "But there's water everywhere."

Then it hit. I didn't know what it was, but it made me groan.

"What's the matter?" Ross asked again.

"I don't know," I answered, a little more concerned now. But whatever it was, it hurt.

"I'm calling the doctor," Ross insisted, springing up from the bed and dashing for the hall telephone.

"Don't do that. What if it's just too much soda pop, a weak bladder, and a bad gas pain? This is embarrassing," I mumbled.

Ross ignored me and made the call.

"Hello. This is Ross Baadsgaard. May I please speak to the doctor? Yes, I realize it's the middle of the night, but my wife's just sprung a leak."

(By way of excuse here, Ross and I had just started our pre-natal classes together, and we hadn't covered water breaking yet. We had passed off breathing exercises like old pros, but we had only attended the first class and still had a little to learn.)

"Yes, I'll hold," I heard Ross answer in the telephone. "Yes, doctor. This is Ross Baadsgaard. What do we do now? Yes. I see. Yes sir. We'll be right over."

Then a major contraction hit, and I moaned from the bathroom. Ross hung up the phone and dashed to the bathroom, his eyes wide and still widening.

"The doctor said to come over to the hospital right away. He said it sounds like your water has broken."

"My what?"

"Your water. You know, the water sac the baby's in. The doctor said the chance for infection is great, and I have to get you right over to the hospital, and he'll check on you there."

I suddenly regretted playing Frisbee in the park the night before. I remembered the dirty dishes in the kitchen sink. I thought about my oily hair and threadbare nightgown.

"I have to take a bath first," I answered. "And get dressed and do the dishes."

"You're *not* doing the dishes. For goodness' sake, Janene, I'm taking you out to the car right now."

"I'm not going anywhere until I have a—" Another contraction. "Moan."

I tried to hold my breath through the pain, then stand up.

"It's impossible," I answered, sitting back down. "I'm leaking all over. I can't go anywhere like this. People will stare at me."

My husband thought for a minute. "I've got it," he said. "You know that disposable diaper they handed out at prenatal class last Tuesday? I'll get that."

"Oh, no!" I answered.

"Wear it," Ross answered, handing me the one and only article of clothing we owned for our little expected one.

He nervously helped me to the car, then charged around to the driver's seat. "How you doing?" he asked as he gunned the engine.

I couldn't answer him. Another contraction was in full force, and I was digging my fingernails into the car seat for support. He sped onto the freeway and headed in the wrong direction. I was absolutely sure my husband was completely turned around and told him so a dozen or more times between moans. He ignored me.

"Do you think we ought to start some breathing exercises?" Ross asked in a rush between stoplights.

He looked over at me. My eyes were bulging out of my head, and I wanted to belt him.

"How can a person be expected to breathe at a time like this?" I finally blurted on a short break between contractions. "That's got to be the dumbest idea anybody ever had."

I don't know how we made it to the hospital, but we did. I sloshed through the emergency room doors and up to the desk.

"Doctor said to bring her over," Ross said in a gush to the nurse at the desk. "Her water's broken."

"Use the elevator on the left and get off on the fifth floor," the nurse said, smiling. "Go to labor and delivery. It'll be on the right once you get off."

As soon as I reached the labor room, a nurse commanded my husband to go back downstairs and check me in. Then she started asking me dumb questions like, "What's your name? What's your doctor's name?"

After about the twenty-seventh question, I sheepishly asked her if I could sit down for a minute. She instructed me to lie down on the labor room table, proceeded to check me, then immediately let out a blood-curdling scream. Screaming is not a reassuring thing to do to a first-time pregnant woman.

"You're already crowned!" she screamed as she ran out of the room. "Don't push! I've got to get a doctor in here!"

Push what? I thought. *I don't want to push anything. I don't think I feel so well.*

There I was, crowned with goodness knows what, and both my nurse and my husband had run out on me. There were no cue cards anywhere. *What do I do now?* I thought. "Heavenly Father," I prayed. "I don't know if I want to do this anymore. I don't know what I'm doing, and everybody else has left me. I'm scared."

A few moments later, a sleepy doctor dragged into the labor

room, rubbing his eyes. He began to check me and then suddenly woke up. "Don't push!" he yelled.

"Don't push!" two more nurses chirped. "Pant, like this," one nurse instructed as she raced me down the hallway, banging into the delivery room doors. The other nurse was busy making weird gasping noises for me to imitate. The doctor threw on a gown and gloves, blasted through the delivery doors, skidded across the room, braked just in front of the delivery table, then lunged toward me just in time to catch.

My husband arrived about this time, looking vaguely like a man from another planet and wearing a white space suit, coming in just in time to hear, "It's a girl."

"Can I push now?" I asked from the table.

"Push what?" the nurse answered.

"Look, Jan," Ross said, rubbing my brow with the back of his palm. "Look, it's a baby. Ohhhh, she's beautiful."

The doctor busied himself taking care of a few loose ends, at least earning a little of his fee, while the nurse wrapped my new daughter in a flannel blanket covered with pink and blue teddy bears, then handed her to my husband.

Ross completely melted, one big six-foot-four-inch, two-hundred-pound puddle of butter right there on the delivery room floor.

"Oh, Jan, she's so soft," he whispered.

For the first time in my life, I was speechless.

When the doctor had finished and they had propped me up a little, Ross gently handed me a tiny, warm, pink body, five pounds of a whole, complete person.

When my husband placed my firstborn daughter gently into my waiting arms, I knew. I loved her more than I could contain. I was a mother. I wanted to sing and dance, blow horns and throw confetti, pray and cry.

"Oh, I love you," I whispered. "I love you. I love you."

I kissed her soft, warm, downy forehead and knew instantly what I was made for. Then my newborn daughter opened her eyes, turned her head, and looked up at me.

"Oh, let this be my heaven," I prayed.

I felt more wonder, more majesty, more love than I had ever felt before. And when my husband put his arms around us and enclosed our first small family, I knew I was hooked for life—and then some.

A Beginning

VIRGINIA H. PEARCE

I was twenty-one years old. It was early autumn, and my husband was beginning his freshman year as a medical student at Creighton University. The city was Omaha. It was a terrifyingly wonderful adventure for someone who had never lived outside of Salt Lake City, Utah. We were on our own—scary and exciting. As the leaves changed color, we shopped for furniture at the local St. Vincent de Paul's. I bought paint and brushes and began to "antique" the end tables while Jim bought anatomy textbooks and began to learn from a cadaver. I enrolled at the University of Nebraska at Omaha, a small campus in the city, to complete the last three quarters of a bachelor's degree.

The days became shorter, life assumed a routine, and we discovered that we were to become parents the next spring. We were thrilled. Neither of us had any notion of what parenthood would mean. I don't recall any conversations concerning it, just a feeling of excitement and anticipation. I had always carried with me a nagging fear that I wouldn't be able to have children, along with a deep desire to be a mother. We had been married only a few months when I felt a deep longing that Jim's and my love for one another be embodied in a child. And now that was to happen.

Winter came to Nebraska. The temperature dropped and the wind blew with a steadiness that chilled us to the bone. Waiting each day on the corner in the early morning dark for the bus, I would read the windchill numbers on the flashing bank sign across the street: -16°, -20°, -4°. Never above zero.

The wind blew, morning sickness subsided, and the new life

within me assumed a visible presence. It began to seem a permanent state: wind and largeness. I dreamed of spring.

At last spring arrived. It came sometime during the week I spent in St. Joseph's Hospital with new little Rosemary—a little bundle of unknown who suddenly made us into a family. In the delivery room I felt like the center of the best party ever. It was like Christmas, where I was both Santa Claus and the little child—all the joys of the giver and all the joys of the receiver.

And then I celebrated my first Mother's Day at St. Joseph's. A Catholic sister came to my room to invite me down for refreshments with the other new mothers. I started to cry and said I would rather not. No, I didn't know what was wrong, and no, I didn't want to talk about it. I didn't want to talk about it, because I didn't know why I felt so sad. I knew that I felt lonely. It was the first time Jim and I had been separated overnight, and when I thought about that, fresh tears would come. I was scared. I realized for the first time that I didn't know anything about babies, and here I had one whose very life depended on me. Furthermore, I probably had no aptitude for learning what I needed to know. I hadn't even liked to baby-sit when I was young.

But worst of all, I felt no real connection to this soft little bundle. Rosemary looked and felt like a complete stranger. She had lots of dark hair. My sister's babies were bald—I think. She had fat, chubby cheeks. The other babies in our family looked skinnier—I think. Whatever the particulars, she didn't look, feel, or sound like anyone I had ever known. When they had placed her in my arms I felt no magical mother-child bond like I had heard women speak of. Maybe I lacked natural affection. That was a curse so profound that I certainly couldn't tell anyone, especially not a calm and serene nun! So I sniffled through lunch and felt waves of guilt because I carried a dark and shameful secret: the absolute knowledge that I was a grossly inadequate mother.

I felt better the next morning, or at least diverted. There were nurses with instruction sheets, papers to be filled out, and a menu from which to order tomorrow's meals. My mother arrived, poured out delight over our little creation, and sat down to visit. Somewhere in the middle of the comfortable chatter, I broached the dark subject: "Should I be feeling something really big? I mean, Mother, she is really cute and cuddly and miraculously healthy, but she doesn't feel like mine!"

Not a ripple of shock, disbelief, or reproach crossed my mother's face. Yes, I was tuned in and looking to see if she would reinforce the inadequacy I felt. Rather, she laughed easily. "Oh," she said, "don't worry about that. It will come. It's what happens when you take care of her day after day after day." That was all she said. And I believed her. I was normal after all.

Time proved that Mother was right. The love happened so quickly and built so fast that I could never imagine again how we could have lived before Rosemary. The next time a baby was handed to me in a delivery room, I was so comfortable in my abilities to attach/bond/love—whatever you call that deep connection between a mother and child—that the anticipation of it provided an immediate reality. I could have sworn I felt it instantly.

What Would You Do?

KATHLEEN "CASEY" NULL

What would you do if you woke up one morning to discover your living space occupied by five other people?

Five other people who

- Perpetually put you last on the shower waiting list; and when there finally is an opening for you it seems as though Macy's Thanksgiving Day parade is marching through the bathroom.
- Become mysteriously magnetized to you when you get a phone call and just as mysteriously disappear when the trash needs to be taken out.
- Suddenly have intense demands: "He's bleeding!", "Where's the checkbook?", "My arm's broken!", "What's for dinner?" just when you're about to have the most profound thought of the century.
- Only let you out when the groceries are gone, to go get more.
- Keep you up late and then get you up early.
- Say that the broccoli and noodle casserole is "yucky" and that they'd rather have UFOs and candied apples.
- Love to draw in the dust or on misty windows but are "allergic" to dusting or window washing.
- Tell you casually where they are going, then go; but expect you to put a bill through Congress if you want to take off for three hours next week.
- Interrupt your thoughts, your conversations, your meals, your showers, and even your sleep.

What would you do?

Probably the same thing I do—you'd stand up in testimony meeting and say that you're grateful for your family.

The Red Shoes

MABEL GABBOTT

The bus seemed to crawl along the streets. Cheryl sat next to the window and counted the blocks. She was on her way to the shoe store to buy some red shoes for Christmas, . . . her first, her very first red shoes. She wriggled her toes inside her old black shoes and thought: "The red ones will be shiny; they will have straps; and they will have silver buckles." Oh, why did the bus have to stop at every corner for all these people! She tapped her finger on the window and waited impatiently.

Mary watched her daughter in tender amusement—amusement because she was recalling how Cheryl had slyly approached her father the night before, saying, "Daddy, you are so wonderful to me. Do you think I could have some new slippers—some red ones?" And she had added, "I really love you so."

Mary's thoughts were tender because she remembered once when she had wanted special slippers so very much—so long ago.

"Mother, this is our corner. Hurry, Mother!"

Cheryl was out in the aisle before the bus stopped.

As they entered the shoe store, Cheryl pointed out to her mother the different styles and colors that were popular.

"What may we do for you?" said the clerk, his eyes smiling at Cheryl.

"Some red shoes, please," said Cheryl, "shiny ones, with a strap."

"Exactly," said the clerk, "exactly what we have just waiting for you on the shelf. I saw the pair this morning and knew you would be along."

The clerk measured Cheryl's foot and brought the slippers. Cheryl took off her old black shoes and slipped her foot into the shiny red slippers. The clerk quickly buckled the strap on the side with the shiny silver buckle. Just then, he was called away for a moment.

"Walk around a little," said Mother, "and see if the shoes fit."

Cheryl walked to the mirror and back. They pinched a little, but no doubt that was just because they were new. She thought, I won't tell about the pinching; there may not be another pair, and I do so want these red ones.

Mary watched her daughter's slight limp as she walked back and forth admiring the shoes in the low mirror.

Suddenly she was a little girl again. It was spring in the little town where she went to school, and she had a part in the spring festival. Mary had gone with her mother to the only store in the town to get white shoes.

"Such a frivolous thing," her mother had said. "White shoes! Should be more sensible. White shoes! You will be cleaning them all the time."

"Oh, I promise I will," Mary had answered.

And in that faraway spring, she remembered, there was one pair of white shoes left—just a little small, but surely they would stretch. She winced inwardly as she tried them on, but smiling to her mother said they were just fine.

That night, Mary remembered, after her mother had tucked her in, turned down the light and said goodnight, Mary had gotten the shoes from the box, found her white stockings, and walked up and down the room trying to stretch the shoes. Finally she went to bed with the shoes still on her feet. Surely in the morning they will have stretched! she thought. But in the morning when her mother wakened her, Mary's little feet were almost numb from the tight shoes, and Mother had to bathe them and rub them and put lotion on them so that she could go to the festival.

But she had worn the white shoes, Mary remembered, hurting with every step as she walked on and off the stage. Foolish indeed, Mary now reflected.

She was drawn from her own childhood memories as the clerk returned.

"They look just beautiful," he said. "How do they feel?"

"Just fine," said Cheryl.

"Cheryl," said Mother, softly, "if they are just a bit too uncomfortable for walking, I am sure the clerk has a pair just a little larger."

"Oh, no!" said Cheryl. "He said this pair on the shelf was waiting just for me."

"Well, now," said the clerk, understanding the situation. "Let me take these back to the manager. Maybe he could stretch them just a little."

Cheryl hesitated, but Mother nodded. She took off the slippers. The clerk returned shortly with another box and another pair of red shoes. Cheryl hesitatingly tried them on. Then she smiled and danced around.

"Oh, they do feel better." She could walk easily and even dance in them.

That night Cheryl modeled her beautiful red slippers for her daddy, while she breathlessly told him about how the slippers had waited on the shelf until she came.

"Oh, you are so good to me, Daddy." She skipped around the room. The red slippers caught the glow of the firelight. "Oh, thank you so much."

"And thank you, Mother." She smiled knowingly to her mother, "Thank you for being so wise."

Mother, Was It I?

BROOKIE PETERSON

When one of our daughters was about eleven years old she seemed depressed and uncooperative. She would say, "You don't love me." We felt frustrated and let down because we thought we had been unwearying in displaying our love to her. One day my husband and I were discussing the situation. I said, "What shall we do?" My husband answered, "Well, perhaps we could use something I learned from dealing with the Aaronic Priesthood boys. If one of them felt this way I wouldn't blame him for not feeling my love. If someone doesn't know that you care for him, you have to assume it's your fault, that you haven't done enough, and you must keep working until he has no doubt that you love him."

I accepted that, though I didn't think our daughter's complaint was justified, considering all we had tried to do for her. But I came to know that it doesn't matter what the parent thinks in this type of situation. If the child doesn't feel loved, you have to double your efforts. So we did. We spent more time with her and tried to be understanding of her feelings. Without going into detail concerning all the ways we attempted to help her, let me explain one thing that was most fruitful.

Soon after our decision to increase our efforts I began a new practice. Almost every evening after our daughter got into bed I went into her room and sat in a little rocking chair near her bed. The light in the room was off, and just a dim light from the hallway filtered into the room. We would visit.

Success didn't come at once; in fact the first evenings were very awkward. She didn't want to visit. But when she learned that at that time I wouldn't scold or preach or give advice, she relaxed her defenses. I would ask about her friends, her school, and her activities. I tried to make those quiet minutes a time for mostly listening on my part. Sometimes I forgot my plan and acted shocked or gave advice; then she would say, "I'm going to sleep now, Mother," and I knew I had lost my chance for that night. It would be a while before she would again trust me to just listen impartially.

We came to love these talks. The other girls kept clamoring for me to sit by their beds also, which I did as best I could. One friend suggested that I sit on the floor while I talked. She said that if I sat at a level lower than my daughter, I would not seem threatening or intimidating. I tried this sometimes; it was a good plan.

Gradually our daughter's attitude changed. In fact it took a period of years, but eventually she seemed to be a different girl, one who was helpful and willing to learn. A most interesting sequel to this story happened years later, when she was about twenty. Because I had thought it might help other parents, I had given this account in some of the talks I gave at stake conferences; she had heard me do this, but we had never discussed it. Once it occurred to me that, though I never used her name in telling the experience, it might be embarrassing to her. So I asked her if my telling this story bothered her. Looking quite surprised she asked, "Mother, was it I?" Then I realized we had had more success than we knew; she didn't even remember the time when she had felt unloved.

Service
and
Compassion

Gentlemen of Mercy

ELAINE CANNON

It is almost the style for people to help people. It is trendy to talk about being a helping hand at the soup kitchen or delivering clothing to central city drop-offs. It seems to be fashionable to be a name on a donor roster, a volunteer schedule, a sign-up sheet for charitable drives, a list for missionary meals. Women bake and take the cake to currently needy members of the neighborhood. Men lend a hand in harvest, a political campaign, a welfare project, and want their names on buildings in exchange for a contribution. Boys and girls paint the widow's window frames, gather the fallen apples, shop for the aged in a glow of organized good deeds. Younger ones read to the blind or the bedridden. It is service, all right, and necessary good deeds are most welcome. Any recipient would count such relief as a blessing. But nothing can touch the sweetness of the work of silent servants whose left hands haven't a clue about what their right hands are doing, who even shudder should mention be made of such service. Anonymity is paramount to such giving, helping people.

There was a gentleman (and the term is used exactly as defined) who had built his fortune through hard work, skill, and prayer. He spent his fortune in surprise service to others. His philosophy was that there are people one would never suspect who are in desperate circumstances. He sought out such situations and gave the surprise service. This gentleman, and others of similar description, brought relief and joy along the way. For example, this "gentleman of mercy" was a guest at a wedding breakfast hosted by a man who had struggled to make a living for his large and fine family. He published a small community newspaper with a small budget. His son had married a girl from an equally large family but with ample means to celebrate in a beautiful way. By the time the groom's family and those on the bride's guest list participated in the wedding breakfast, the cost had soared. A giving gentleman guest had learned that the host had borrowed on his insurance to fund the festivity.

Some readers might urge a lesson on living within one's means, but few of us know the inside workings of a family. The facts are that this was a crisis situation, and a bill had to be paid. The father stood waiting to pay the bill when the gentleman of mercy came and said the father was needed back with the family for photographs. With the father gone, the gentleman paid the bill, with strict instructions not to reveal his identity. The father wept when he learned he had no bill to pay, and repeatedly said, "God bless the giver!"

Another gentleman of mercy quietly bought a van for a handicapped man who would no longer need to be a shut-in, and whose caregiving wife struggled to provide for both of them. For them it was a life-changing miracle; yet others had never perceived their need. Another gentleman of mercy sent a cashier's check for thousands of dollars to a local medical facility for services rendered a young automobile accident victim, whose severe injuries and subsequent financial obligations had pressed the family toward bankruptcy. It was a small thing to the giver, perhaps, but to the victim's bishop-father it was an enormous blessing and wondrous, humbling evidence of God's caring.

There was a prominent man who had earned great financial success in life. All along the way he abundantly gave to others. Then, just before his retirement years, a crisis struck his life. Because of circumstances beyond his control, he lost his fortune, his home, his self-esteem. He fought to right the wrongs, and when word of this great man's situation was whispered about in the community, people rushed to his aid and fought to underwrite a fund-raising banquet in his honor. He was rich with grateful friends; he was the beneficiary of silent servants who did not forget blessings they had known through him.

No doubt about it, counting the blessing of silent servants of God is an awakening of the heart.

$\mathcal{L}$earning to Receive

ANN W. ORTON

Only one errand to do on Friday—please, Mom, find me a book at the library, my oldest daughter requested as she raced out the door for class. Not that challenging, I reasoned. I could drive to the library and check out a book in my present condition. A few controlled minutes in public seemed possible, but I'd keep the tissue box close by in case another unsuspected event triggered an untimely flow of tears.

I drove to the city library, delighted to find two adjacent parallel parking spaces. After parking the car without incident, I began the search for the book. The card catalog announced the classification numbers, even the floor location, so I ambled along to the escalator. No tissues required as yet. Once in the stacks, I began the search for the title. I looked for five minutes, counting number to number in vain. I was in the correct spot; why was the book missing? Without warning, the flood of frustration set off the tears and I began to cry. Before long I was crying uncontrollably, sobbing and searching for a tissue, not a title. Finally my wailing attracted the attention of a library employee who came to my rescue. She ushered me into the restroom and tried to uncover the source of my dismay. I gave her the standard Mormon mom reply—"I'm just fine"—as I endeavored to regain my composure. Reassured that I wasn't immediately suicidal, she left me to my puddles and swelling eyes.

Why was I crying? What caused me to lose control of my emotions over such a simple thing as a missing book? Another episode like this, I reasoned, and I'd be locked up. In fact, I considered driving myself directly to the emergency room for assistance. But a brief reality check reminded me that Emily, my grade school daughter, would be home shortly and be locked out of the house if I weren't there. I left the library empty-handed and red-eyed, found my car, and drove back home without the book. I had failed one more time.

The library encounter was only one of many emotional collapses following the departure of my husband of 22 years. After several years in a roller coaster relationship, he left for the final time. We had recently relocated to Salt Lake City after a five-year assignment in North Carolina. We moved into our new home and went through all the motions of being a healthy, functional family. We even managed to present our family "welcome to the ward" introductions in sacrament meeting.

On the Sunday after we spoke in church, I sat alone on the pews and cried through the meetings. A concerned sister approached me after a drippy hour and asked if she could help. I dabbed at my eyes and explained that I was "just fine," and she moved on through the crowd. Much to my surprise, she called later in the day to check again. Then she called every day with a message of concern and support. I dutifully persisted that I was "just fine," not yet ready to unburden my real concerns on a stranger.

After the library scene, I recognized that "just fine" was blatantly inaccurate. I was immersed in emotional turmoil, and I had no idea how to begin the climb out. I finally called my neighbor and told her my husband had left us. She came over, but not before she'd called her physician husband and arranged a counseling appointment for me. Carol took care of Emily, my grade school daughter, left a note for the other children, then drove me to the doctor's office. She waited for me during the session, then drove me home once again, a procedure she continued throughout the following week. As the long days turned into weeks, my supportive and loving neighbor continued to share time and energy with me.

I finally admitted that only complete desperation had motivated me to call Carol after the library collapse. After all,

I reasoned, I was an educated and capable woman. I lived the commandments, attended my meetings, served in the ward, studied my scriptures, and said my prayers. I thought I'd done what I should do to solve the problems I was facing, but I was sinking lower and lower. I recognized that a solution to my problems was beyond my individual resources. Even my pleadings with the Lord often seemed unheard, but it was I who couldn't comprehend the answers he sent.

In my struggles, I consistently overlooked a basic premise of the gospel taught by the Savior: service to our brothers and sisters is synonymous with service to our Heavenly Father (see Matthew 25:35–45). Rendering service to those in need constructs the underpinnings of a ward family unit. Oh, I knew this principle from years of service to others, but what I failed to understand was the significance of the principle in reverse. Service to our Heavenly Father is two-dimensional: we give *and* we receive.

The Pahoran Principle

MARILYNNE TODD LINFORD

In my first few months as a Relief Society president, I wanted to meet every sister in the ward. (I'm sure many Relief Society presidents have that same desire.) I wasn't expecting a red carpet at every door. I knew there would be some who would just be polite. I even expected some wouldn't answer the door and others would not invite us in.

At this time I happened to read Alma 59–61 in the Book of Mormon. These chapters refer to Moroni's letters to Pahoran, the chief governor of the land. Moroni's armies were suffering greatly from the need of support. In Moroni's first letter, he asked Pahoran for men and supplies. When Pahoran did not respond, Moroni sent a chastisement and a second request. He accused Pahoran of neglect, thoughtlessness, slothfulness, idleness, trying to usurp power, and even possible treason. Moroni told Pahoran that the judgments of God would fall upon him. He threatened to leave the area he was in and go to Zarahemla to fight against Pahoran and the government unless his needs were met. Moroni falsely accused Pahoran. After making Moroni aware of his own precarious situation Pahoran said, "In your epistle you have censured me, but it mattereth not; I am not angry, but do rejoice in the greatness of your heart" (Alma 61:9). This is the Pahoran principle of service—no matter what, keep cool, respond with understanding, and look for the greatness of heart.

Okay, I have just read about Moroni and Pahoran, verbalized the principle, and now I go out visiting. I knock on a door (my counselor is with me). The door opens enough for two eyes to look out at us. "Who are you?" the woman asks in an angry tone.

"I am your Relief Society president," I begin to say. She yells, "I don't have or need a Relief Society president." I feel like yelling back, "Okay for you" and want to shake the dust off my feet. But remembering Pahoran, I move closer, put my foot in the door, and say, "You don't need a Relief Society president? Tell me why." "Well, I just don't. They always get in the way, try to clean your house or something."

At this point my counselor hands me the treats we brought for our sister. "I promise never to get in the way, and no one will come clean your house," I say, feeling shaky, "because it looks like it doesn't need it. Here are a few goodies we brought for you." She opens the door all the way. "Well, come in and hear what I have to say," she demands. With trepidation, we enter. I set the treats on her table. She tells us she doesn't need us, that we should never come again, that we are bigots, liars, and misguided pawns of our husbands and Church authorities.

I use all the Pahoran techniques I can remember. I tell her that we are happy to meet her. We compliment her on her home and thank her for taking time for us. I try to see the greatness of her heart.

Little by little over the next many months, she begins to trust us. We discover the cause of her bitterness. We discover she has a sense of humor. We give her a whatever/whenever coupon. We take her shopping. She calls several times when something needs fixing. She seems to enjoy our visits, and we enjoy her fun, say-it-like-it-is personality. We see that service, the Pahoran style, works.

Service Becomes Less of a Sacrifice

MICHAELENE GRASSLI

One daughter felt prompted—she says compelled by the Spirit—to attend a meeting in which I was speaking to Primary leaders. She recalls that during the talk she had a specific feeling of comfort envelop her. She realized that her sacrifice of not always having her mother available to her was important because Primary was important. When she was called as a counselor in her stake Primary two days later, it was made known to her that her call was because of her own qualifications and worthiness, not because of her mother.

Experiences such as these are verification to me that the Lord is more than fair. He expects us to serve, and he helps and blesses us and those around us when we do. Our service makes us worthy of his blessings, which, if we recognize them, bring us great joy.

Now, when we recognize our blessings, something very significant happens: *The service we give seems less of a sacrifice.* We aren't serving out of duty and counting the things we give up. We are serving mostly because we love to do it. It feels good. We want to keep doing what feels good. This is when we begin to understand the concept of true consecration. It ceases being a sacrifice because what we may give up seems unimportant when compared with the way we feel when we serve.

We are serving because we love the Lord.

Just Make Him Stop

NAME WITHHELD

A few of us were discussing the trials of raising children. The focus turned to one lady in the group who had just discovered her son was using drugs. She was, of course, completely distraught and didn't have a clue as to what to do next. With my great expertise (my oldest was nine years of age), I spoke up. "Why don't you just make him stop?" She looked at me with such sadness and said, "It just doesn't work that way."

A few years later I was having some serious trouble with a teenager. This very same lady called me. (I have always been impressed that not once did she say, "I told you so.") She said, "If you ever need a shoulder to cry on, remember, I've been there." Whenever I see someone sorrowing over a stray child, I try to remember her example.

One Winter's Night

DAVID O. McKAY

One winter's night many years ago in a humble country home in a little town in Utah a mother was taken sick. Three children sat around a table in a room lighted by an old-fashioned coal-oil lamp. The father was away from home on business. The mother, who had been ill during the day, had taken a turn for the worse. The nearest doctor was twelve miles distant through a canyon. There was no telephone communication and no other practical means of reaching the doctor that night. The mother said to the eldest child, a lad of six or seven, "I think you had better go to Sister Smith's and ask her if she will please come over for a while."

The lad crossed the street to the barn, bridled his pony and rode through the newly fallen snow four or five blocks distant. Mrs. Smith was alone attending to household duties in the kitchen. When she heard that the lad's mother was ill, she took off her apron, stepped into the bedroom, presumably to see that her own little ones were snug and comfortable, threw a shawl over her head and shoulders and traipsed along in the steps of the lad's pony, holding her skirts as best she could to keep them from trailing in the snow.

Arriving in the home, she rendered such service to the ailing mother as only skilled and willing hands can give. The children were ushered to bed and were soon asleep, unmindful of the number of hours that Mrs. Smith spent at the bedside of the stricken woman.

The lad grew to manhood before he realized the beauty and significance of that little incident—a mother acting in the role of an angel of mercy.

I relate this because in simplicity it illustrates the highest and best in Woman's Realm—home making and compassionate service.

The Day We Picked the Beans

MABEL GABBOTT

That summer was the most prolific bean summer we could remember. Every morning Mama said, "Up early now and see if there are any beans ready for canning." There always were. Day after day, we picked early, and we canned during the morning hours. When the best of the beans were bottled, and the picking grew thinner and thinner, we began to nod conspiratorily at one another. Bean canning was done for another summer.

Then one day Mama looked across the road to the Evans's bean patch.

"I do believe she needs help," she said.

That evening Mama went over to see Marie. They walked through the garden, talking and pinching and nodding. We watched and sighed.

It wasn't that Marie wasn't just as energetic as Mama (she was even younger), and ever so hardworking (she worked downtown each day), or that she needed the canned beans any the less for her family (she had little children). It was just that Mama had a terrific green thumb, a deep respect for any growing thing, and a horror of waste. She couldn't let those beans get one day older or tougher.

The next morning, earlier than usual, there was Mama.

"Up, everyone!" she called cheerily, "We are picking beans today."

"But, Mama," we hesitated. "Ours are all in bottles."

"The Evans's beans are not," said Mama. "Up now, quickly!"

We carried Marie's bottles across the road to our kitchen and scalded them. We picked basket after basket of beans. We sat on our screened back porch and snapped beans.

Mama was in the hot kitchen, canning them as fast as we had some ready. It didn't matter that we thought some were too old. They would be nourishing when summer greens were gone, Mama explained.

When Marie came home, after gathering up her little children, she found her bean patch harvested and bottles and bottles of beans to store against a cold white winter.

We grumbled as we stooped to pick the beans, and we groaned as we swished away summer flies while we snapped the beans; but being young and experienced in sharing such family ventures, we sang songs and shared stories as bean after bean found its way into its winter storage place.

And somehow now when I think of our small town and our screened back porch, of summer gardens and Mama, I think of that day we picked our neighbor's beans. And each time I remember, my mother grows wiser and dearer.

"Silver and Gold Have I None; But Such As I Have Give I Thee"

H. BURKE PETERSON

Some of us may not understand what we really mean by service. This principle is illustrated by an experience that two of the early Apostles had after the Savior was resurrected. It is found in the book of Acts. Peter and John were going into the temple through the gate called Beautiful, and as they passed through the gate there sat a man who had been lame since he was born. He looked up and held out his hand, asking for alms; he was begging.

> And Peter, fastening his eyes upon him with John, said [speaking to the lame man], Look on us.
>
> And he gave heed unto them, expecting to receive something of them.
>
> Then Peter said, Silver and gold have I none; but such as I have give I unto thee: In the name of Jesus Christ of Nazareth rise up and walk.
>
> And he [meaning Peter] took him by the right hand, and lifted him up. (Acts 3:4–7.)

With these words Peter gave us another secret. As you think of service to others, remember the words, "Silver and gold have I none; but such as I have give I thee."

Some time ago I was attending a stake conference in the United States. The stake president met me at the airport, and we had an hour's drive to the stake center. As we were driving we talked about many things, and the conversation began to center on an individual who lived in the stake. The stake president told me about a young lady who had gone on a mission about twenty years before, and while there had contracted polio. She walked into the hospital in a city in New England to take some tests, and she never walked again. She was paralyzed. And he said, "For twenty years she's been paralyzed from her neck down; she's not able to move any muscles below her neck, except a few in her fingers. But she's an unusual young lady. She has a spirit that is something wonderful." Well, before stake conferences I always get a little nervous. Consequently I said, "I need to be built up, President; let's go by and see the young lady."

So we went by her home; she was living with her parents. We went into her room, and there she lay on a bed, surrounded by the equipment that would keep her interested and busy during the day. As I walked into the room, I saw a physically pitiful sight, but I felt a spirit that I have felt in very few places. I was overcome by her spirit. I began to ask her some questions. As she lay there I saw that she could move a few fingers on one hand and a few on the other, but she could not raise or lower her arms. She had an air pump on a table by her side. She would hold the tube in her hand and every few minutes would put it into her mouth. It would blow air into her lungs. She would then turn away and her lungs would deflate. She did this several times an hour to keep the air moving into her body. And I said, "Tell me what you do during the day." I knew she had lain there for twenty years in this physical condition.

And her parents said, "We'll show you how she spends her days."

They brought a typewriter and put it in front of her on her bed. Her mother laid one hand on the typewriter keys, then she took the other and also laid it on the keys. The young lady then showed us how with these few fingers she would type. She said, "During the day I find those who are sick and discouraged and write poetry and letters to them and send them good wishes that will make them happy. I try to help those who are less fortunate than I am." There she lay with hardly anything physical going for her, but with a spirit that could perform miracles.

Next her parents brought a telephone and put it in her hands and moved it up to her ear and mouth. With two fingers, she punched the push-button dial. In this way she called those who were not as well off as she was and cheered them up during the day. Remember what Peter said: "Silver and gold have I none; but such as I have give I thee."

$\mathcal{S}$tatistics of Service

MARILYNNE TODD LINFORD

$\mathbf{M}$y incredible, multi-talented friend Laurie Hansen wrote a letter to the editor:

My husband was diagnosed with colon cancer eighteen months ago and died this month at the age of forty-four. I was unable to keep track of visits, phone calls, and many expressions of love. But I did write down acts of kindness, which may seem insignificant by themselves but can mount up to immense support.

During the last eighteen months we received over 100 meals, 125 plates of bakery goods, and over 500 cards or letters of good wishes. Approximately 270 people have donated money, 70 have given gifts, and over 300 people have contributed toward flowers. I kept track of at least 375 acts of time/labor. The people I work with donated over 130 hours of vacation time so that I could be with Greg while he was alive. People we didn't even know gave us a condominium in Hawaii for a week, and others gave us the money for the rest of the trip. A beach house, tickets, rooms at Disneyland, and airline tickets for our entire family, along with spending money to enjoy two full weeks in southern California were given last year so that our five daughters could enjoy their father while he still felt well. A home in St. George was provided for several quick getaways. At the time Greg was diagnosed we were in the middle of building an addition on our home. Many came to help him complete the task he had started.

I figure that if every person who sent a card, meal, or treat prayed once a day for us over the last eighteen months, that equals 396,575 prayers! I'd like to thank everyone from the bottom of my heart. You have pulled me through hard times and instilled in me a love for mankind for which I will be forever grateful.

Happiness, even in adversity, is counting blessings.

$\mathcal{S}$ister Anderson

BARBARA B. SMITH

What I could not learn in the classroom about the Relief Society's work of love, I very soon began to learn from compassionate service provided by visiting teaching, in which women are sent two by two to visit sisters in the ward each month. President Kimball said that when the Lord needs to answer prayers, he sends us to do the task; often it is visiting teachers who receive those assignments.

My companion and I were assigned to visit a couple who had just moved onto the back side of our circle. We were happy to accept that assignment, but when we knocked at the door and stood there for a few minutes before it opened, we felt perhaps we had come at a difficult time. A lovely woman, with black hair pulled back into a bun, opened the door. She was neat and comely, but very businesslike. We introduced ourselves and welcomed her to the neighborhood. Then before we left, we told Sister Anderson that we would come again the next month. She gave very little response.

The next month we did go back again, and that time Sister Anderson had her arm in a sling. She said that she had fallen while putting away some of her household items and had broken her arm. We asked if we might be of service, but she abruptly told us that she was a professional nurse and was certain that she could manage.

The third month came around and when Sister Anderson came to the door, again we were left standing on the porch as she informed us that her husband was confined to bed. He had suffered a stroke. Again she assured us that she was capable of taking care of him and of herself. It seemed to me that there was a bitterness in her that turned people from their door. The months passed with regular front-porch visits and then, on one occasion, I needed to take my baby with me. This time, though reluctantly at first, and almost with anxious concern, Sister Anderson invited us to come in. She said her husband had become very lonely and needed to talk to someone other than her, day after day. She thought he would like to see the baby. She opened the door, and for the first time, we went into that home.

From then on I took the baby with me when we went to see the Andersons. We were delighted to find in this child a common ground that seemed to make our calls more acceptable. Smiles began to appear when we came instead of the stern countenance we first saw.

We became good friends and had pleasant visits, but my companion and I could feel that they did not want the message. One time, however, it was on love. I thought anyone could talk about love, but I learned it was perhaps the most difficult subject of all for them. Apparently the children of Brother Anderson had been very much opposed to the remarriage of their father after their mother had passed away. The hurtful things that were said and done had created feelings of bitterness and resentment. We were sorry to learn of the unhappy experiences, but the sharing of them seemed to create a bond of trust between us.

One day my telephone rang, and it was Sister Anderson asking me if I could help her find someone to cut the lawn. I knew several young boys and sent one over immediately. Later, she called to tell me that her husband was sick again. She needed to get to the store and asked if I could help her. I did. When her husband passed away she asked for our counsel about the services and for help she needed with his personal affairs. I can't adequately express the happiness that came to me, knowing that she felt confident enough to call. She started to come out to our meetings and was really loved and accepted, and I know she felt it.

The most thrilling thing for me was to go home one afternoon and find a card in my screen door, with her name signed to it as one of my visiting teachers. It wasn't that way with every experience, but at least in this instance, knowing that we had helped to make Sister Anderson's life more tolerable, more purposeful, and a bit less stressful for her, gave me a feeling of warmth. I found myself facing each day with a little more purpose.

*L*et's Do Your Hair

ELAINE CANNON

Several Relief Society sisters went to the hospital to visit a cancer patient who was failing so fast that she didn't have any will to live. Donna Conkling (one of the famous King Sisters) swept into the room, glamorous, perfumed, coiffed, and went over to the bed and stood next to the patient.

"Turn this way, dear," Donna soothed. "Let's do your hair."

The pale lips smiled weakly as Donna sat down on the bed and cradled her friend as she brushed through the tumbled locks.

One woman brought flowers; one brought warm words of comfort; but Donna brushed the sinking woman's hair.

My experience is that the good news of the gospel makes people do things they wouldn't otherwise do. They are inspired by Christ's example, his mission, and the restoration of the fulness of the gospel. Suddenly we begin to enjoy a bit of heaven now.

Faith
and
Hope

ℒet Your Hearts
Be Comforted

KRIS MACKAY

Trusting the scriptures became a habit early in the life of JoAnn Barrett Gray.

The oldest of a sizeable family, she remembers how her parents gathered all eleven children around the table in their farmhouse in Idaho, how under her father's direction they searched out and studied the holy words of God.

The amazing thing to JoAnn as a child was how often her parents picked the very scripture to solve a problem in their children's lives. Their knowledge of exactly where to find counsel a family member needed was impressive.

JoAnn and Gary continued turning to the scriptures regularly in their own home, with their own three children—Christine, small, dark-haired, with a keen, serious mind like her father's; Steven, strong, sturdy, all boy; and Marilyn, tall, willowy, with hair as fair as her sister Christine's was dark. Three so different in appearance, and yet each one so dear.

When the children were very small JoAnn and Gary read them stories from the Bible. As teenagers they opened their own books around the table after dinner. Each took his or her turn speaking the words aloud, and then lively discussions pinpointed how they felt about what they had read. These were priceless hours of closeness and love.

All too soon the children grew up, married, and moved away, establishing their own homes and starting their own little families.

Sadly, none of us is immune to tragedy. In November 1984

Christine lost her valiant fight with cancer, a struggle she waged for eighteen months and at one point seemed to have won. In the end she left not only her grieving parents and brother and sister, but a desolate husband and three helpless babies, the youngest a scant two years old.

Stunned with grief, JoAnn and Gary clung together and held tightly to their faith as to a lifeline. Losing Christine was almost impossibly hard to bear, but with God's help they would learn to accept it.

Five months later their grief was compounded by truly unbelievable news. Steven had been killed—instantly—in a car crash.

Psychiatrists warn that the gravest danger associated with stress is heaping a second tragedy onto the first, without opportunity to properly heal. Two of their three children were gone— in only five short months! Was that *possible?* Neighbors and friends worried that the double blow might be more than the Grays could handle, and if they buckled under the load, who could blame them?

Yet somehow they did handle it. Keeping busy helped. Throwing themselves into their jobs during the week and into Church callings on Sundays filled enough of the void that at least they could walk through the motions of living, to keep up appearances. Perhaps, in time, some measure of inner comfort would return.

On April 21, 1985, a month after Steven's accident, JoAnn told herself she had buried her sorrow reasonably well, considering.

It was Sunday. She dutifully attended ward conference in one of the sister wards, in her capacity as Young Women secretary in the stake.

She drove home after the meeting was over, arriving before her husband did, and stepped into a house that was empty—and silent—and cold.

Unfortunately, not quite empty. Sorrow lurked behind the front door and its presence overwhelmed her completely, attacking so suddenly and viciously that she was powerless to fight it off alone.

With a fresh burst of agony every bit as raw as it had been in the beginning, JoAnn faced honestly the loneliness of life without two of her children, and acknowledged for the first time that the comfort she yearned for with her whole soul had not come.

Her pain was so overwhelming that she threw herself on the bed, arms stretched out, sobs racking her body, and cried in anguish, "Oh, my children, my children! How can I go on without you?"

Finally, when the worst of the hysteria passed, she knelt in great weariness at the side of the bed in prayer. She pleaded for only one thing.

"Heavenly Father, I have always tried to do what you would ask of me. Now I am desperate and I need your help. I *need* some assurance that Christine and Steven are with you, that they are happy and well. Please, *please* let them come to me for just a minute. Let me feel their touch just once—*please* Father—that in my mother's heart I might know they are all right."

In this attitude of humility she waited, motionless, alert, for a lengthy period of time, willing the veil to part enough for some small contact.

Nothing happened. Nothing at all.

Exhausted, JoAnn rose to her feet, not bitter, but understanding instinctively that the miracle she begged for would not be hers. She must—and perhaps even could—endure to the end on the basis of the faith she already had.

But because the habit was ingrained, she groped on the nightstand for her scriptures. She would read to pass the time until Gary's car sounded in the driveway.

The volume fell open in her hands. Not to the front or center pages as books usually do when moving naturally on their own, but close to the end. Her eyes still brimmed with tears as she blinked and tried to focus on the words:

"Therefore, let your hearts be comforted concerning Zion; for all flesh is in mine hands; be still and know that I am God" (D&C 101:16).

Be still and know that I am God! That was her answer. Her

children were all right, in a heaven where those who have passed on are busy and well, and she was filled with the inexpressible comfort of that knowledge.

She no longer needs to waste time searching for answers to questions that are already answered.

Heavenly Father is taking care of us all.

Answered Prayer

SUSAN EVANS McCLOUD

Little one, I prayed for you before the time you came.
Aren't a waiting mother's prayers always the same?
Let this child be healthy, please let him be all right!
A woman's anguished pleadings into the silent night.

Then you came; not healthy, but more perfect than I knew,
I wondered what the Lord had done, sending me you.
What about my foolish prayers, had they all been in vain?
He had listened, knowing He was sending me pain.

It took a while to understand, a while to see
What a blessing heaven had held in store for me.
I had wanted something less, not knowing you were there,
Nor all the tender love that stood behind my answered prayer.

$\mathcal{R}$eturning
Good for Evil

ELAINE CANNON

Judy Thompson said her family was not stricken by war or public bombings but that their suffering nonetheless had been acute. When their problems began they were living in a small Ohio town where everyone went to the one and only Protestant church to play bingo on Saturday nights for pocket change; then back they'd go again on Sunday to worship. Usually the same people showed up for both occasions, and Judy's family was part of that crowd. Then Judy's husband, Brett, met a fine man who was a bank loan officer in a larger city nearby. Brett was trying to get a loan to build an addition to their house. The twin girls were nearly ten years old now and needed a room apart from their older brother. Mr. Rawson asked Brett many questions about his life, his values, his family. Approved, Brett received the loan. In addition, the two men found that they had much in common, and before long the Thompson family was driving over to the Rawson home each week to meet with the LDS missionaries for gospel instruction. They even attended church services in that city a time or two before they were baptized. As often as they could, the Thompsons happily drove the distance to the city for church with the Mormons.

Soon the trouble began among their neighbors in the small town where they lived. Resentment built up over their conversion. The children were not welcome in the homes of their friends, and they were beaten up at school. Robert even lost his job as delivery boy for the pharmacist. Brett and Judy were not invited to social events; they couldn't even get appointments at the barber and beauty shop! The gas station wouldn't service the car. The owner of the grocery store deliberately turned his back and walked away when any of the family came in for supplies. It was a miserable time. The only thing that had changed was their understanding of God and the plan of life, and yet no one—not a soul—would speak to any family member.

"We cried out to the Lord to show us the way," Judy said. "We clung to each other and made excuses for our neighbors. We put our house up for sale, and garbage was thrown on the porch. Rocks broke our windows. Imagine that kind of prejudice in this day and age. We wondered what we had gotten ourselves into.

"The children wanted to give up this new church because their friends had told them that was the problem. It was truly awful," added Judy. "A spirit of darkness and despair was surrounding us all. At first we were too embarrassed to mention our problem to our new Mormon friends at the church in the city where Brett now worked."

Judy continued, "One day the bishop drove all the way out to our home to keep an appointment. He told us about the people in Alma's day who had suffered so greatly at the hands of their enemies. When they couldn't stand it any longer, he said, they began to cry out mightily to God, just as we had been doing. The bishop had us turn to our scriptures and read the following passage from Mosiah 24:13–15: 'And it came to pass that the voice of the Lord came to them in their afflictions, saying: Lift up your heads and be of good comfort, for . . . I will . . . ease the burdens which are put upon your shoulders, that even you cannot feel them upon your backs, even while you are in bondage; . . . The burdens which were laid upon [them] were made light; yea, the Lord did strengthen them that they could bear up their burdens with ease, and they did submit cheerfully and with patience to all the will of the Lord.'"

Judy's story ended with a beautiful testimony. The bishop called their attention to the next verses in that chapter, which reminded this fine family that God does visit his people in their afflictions. They are not forgotten. This he does because of covenants made and also so that they will be witnesses to others of God's goodness!

Judy's family knelt in prayer, and the bishop asked Heavenly Father to protect each family member and to bless the home. He asked that they might be guided with ideas about appropriate ways to rebuild friendships so that hearts in the town could be softened and the work of the Lord could go forward.

Judy said, "We continued to return good for evil and to do all kinds of Christian service, like getting up early to secretly shovel a neighbor's pathways or to chop wood for a widow's wood-burning stove or to make tiny cakes for a wedding we were not invited to. We now know four other people who have seen the missionaries and have been baptized. We *know* that the Lord lives and answers prayers. We are witnesses to that. We are happier than ever before now."

We do not know what we have to go through to get where we are meant to be! Heavenly Father yearns for our success in life and our safe return to his presence.

No doubt about it, one blessing to be grateful for is this knowledge of God's love for his covenant children. Regardless of what we suffer or how we are tried, he will help us and we can then be humble witnesses of him, for we know things that other people don't know yet!

$\mathcal{I}$ Will Wait for Spring

JANENE WOLSEY BAADSGAARD

She was carrying hot turkey soup and chocolate-striped cookies on a china plate when she knocked at my door.

"How are you feeling?" she asked. "I've brought some warm soup for your lunch."

She walked into my kitchen and set the homemade soup and cookies on the counter. Then she turned to me.

"I'm so sorry," she said. "When something bad happens to someone you love, you feel like you're going through it with them."

She hugged me. I could feel the soft fur collar on her coat and the warmth of her cheek against mine.

"I love you," she whispered in my ear.

We walked slowly toward the door.

"I was going to ask you," she continued. "Is a miscarriage like having a baby, with the pain and all?"

Then it all came flooding back. The past month in and out of bed with spotting, cramping, and uncertainty. Then there was the sudden hemorrhage, the hurried call to the doctor, the rushed trip to the emergency room, the stirrups, IV, blood, nausea, contractions, the doctor too busy watching a basketball game to come in time, the nurse carrying warm blankets, the worried husband with his firm palm on my moist forehead.

"Yes," I answered. "It's like having a baby. It *is* having a baby . . . too soon."

My husband took off his coat to keep me warm on the drive home from the emergency room that black February night. He cradled my head in his lap, his arms shaking with the cold. When we arrived home, he carried me from the car to the bedroom, quietly closed the door, and tried to explain to our other children what had happened.

The next day, when I wanted to belt the doctor who wouldn't leave the basketball game, scream at my other children for still needing to be fed, and tear the wash that still needed to be done, my husband took me in his arms until the shaking and sobbing eased. Then he fixed supper for the children and took care of the mountain of washing.

"Mommy?" my four-year-old son, Joseph, asked me later that night. "Did our baby die?"

"Yes, honey," I answered.

"But you were supposed to take your vitamins so our baby wouldn't die," Joseph said.

"I did take my vitamins," I answered. "But our baby died anyway."

"I wanted our baby to be a boy so I could play with him in the backyard," Joseph said.

"I know, honey," I answered. "I wanted our baby too."

Joseph pulled his eyebrows together and thought for a long time.

"Maybe Heavenly Father will save another baby for us," Joseph said, his face brightening.

"I hope so, Joseph," I answered. "I hope so."

Weeks later, an ache in my center lingered, a feeling there was no inside of me. Snow was falling that morning. I hadn't been out of the safe, warm cocoon of my home since it happened. It seemed wrong of the world to just keep going along with all the usual things. I wanted everything and everyone to stop for a moment and let me say good-bye. But there were still carpet cleaning salesmen on the telephone, dishes to wash, and garbage cans to be brought in from the street.

It was cold outside, cold and threatening. I forced myself to push my feet inside my boots and trudge out to the street. I grabbed a smashed garbage can in each hand, then headed for the gate of the fence enclosing our backyard.

Swinging the gate wide, I sidestepped through the opening into the backyard, kicking the gate closed behind me. The snow lay unsoiled and untouched before me, changing everything into something new, clean, and white.

I walked slowly to the back of the house, dragging the cans at my sides. The sun was setting and gave the snow a warm glow. An icicle, hanging precariously from the roof, broke off and shattered like broken glass on the snow crust below. The air was hushed and silent.

I caught my breath and held it. My eyes stung. For the first time in a long while, I was able to look at the world in awe, overcome with the beauty around me.

A sense of reverence swept over me as I walked where no one had walked before. The sun slowly sank lower in the western sky, and I saw the color of the snow change from a warm, golden glow to a clear, cool blue.

The new year was upon me with all the unknown way I had to go. But I knew I had to say good-bye before I could say hello. I saw the gentle earth lying beneath the drifts of snow, submissive to the trust the seasons keep. I felt reborn to the miracle of the cycle of loss and gain, darkness and light, life and death.

"Good-bye," I whispered in the stillness. "I will wait for spring."

Bill

NAME WITHHELD

After my son Bill returned from his mission he committed a serious transgression, and because of embarrassment and other factors he became inactive and alienated. There had been much prayer and fasting by his family on his behalf. Nevertheless, he still shied away from the Church or anything to do with it.

One day, as I was praying, I felt strongly that Bill was struggling within himself and needed help. "Perhaps," I thought, "if he had a little push from the Lord it might help." So I began to pray and fast specifically for him. Within a few days, his bishop and his stake president came to visit him. When Bill commented on the rarity of having both of them visit, he was told, "It is the practice of the stake leaders to meet periodically and go through the list of less-active members, to kneel as a group and pray about who they should visit, and to list in order of consideration five names to be visited." The first name on every leader's list that day was my son Bill. I was grateful that my prayer had been answered in a most discernible manner.

Coins

JEAN CHAPIN SEIFERT

Little one,
remember when I took
the five brown pennies
from your hand,
and in their place
I put a gleaming silver dime?
To my surprise,
you cried with rage—
replacing five with one
could not be fair!

I smiled, then,
at childish reckoning . . .
until I thought how often
that our Father takes away
the copper blessings
from my hand
and in their place
He puts more precious ones.
Yet, angrily, I count myself
defrauded by the gift.

I have not understood
Eternal reckoning.

The Mountain That Moved (Almost)

KRIS MACKAY

The mountains that range across France, Switzerland, and Italy are rugged. The Alps rise abruptly from level ground to towering peaks, and their twisting hairpin turns are challenging. Gentle, rolling foothills graduating upward are unknown in that part of the world.

Closed in winter when snow blocks their passes, the roads are next to impossible for novices to navigate, even in summer.

My sister Dolores, who prefers to be called Lori, didn't know that.

Lori Hitchcock and her son picked up their shiny new Volkswagon bug at the Brussels Airport in Belgium. They piled a tent and other camping gear in and around the tiny, red automobile and they were ready to go.

Mark had turned eighteen and it seemed to Lori to be the perfect opportunity to spend quality hours alone with him. Another year or less and Mark would be grown up and gone.

Now, while he balanced almost across the tightrope between boyhood and transformation into a man, they would camp along the scenic byways of Europe with time for leisurely conversations and the formation of golden memories neither would ever forget.

This was their first trip to Europe. Neither spoke the languages indigenous to the countries on their schedule, but that didn't worry them. Lori teaches high school math and is trained to be practical. She was confident they could handle what Europe presented.

It was glorious summer! Mark reveled in freedom after high school graduation, and Lori was likewise free to fill her hours as she pleased. Adventure beckoned more compellingly with every turn of the wheels.

A colorful map propped on the dashboard kept them on course. Prominent red lines marked the main, super highways, but those they ignored. They preferred sights that lay off the beaten track.

They wanted to meet farmers toiling in their fields and to listen to street vendors in picturesque villages singing out their wares, peddling hot sausages to be eaten with buns, or chestnuts heated over an open fire.

Single purple lines on the map directed them to the second best highways. Double purple was reserved for rougher roads, and the yellow line indicated those that were barely passable. They chose the single purple, or second best.

The map guided them reliably through Germany and Switzerland during a succession of exciting days and beautiful nights. They marvelled at small haystacks individually perched on short wooden poles in fields resembling a horde of invading Martians. Once they pulled off the road to savor fresh peanuts thrown into a homemade kettle and swirled through hot, bubbling toffee. Europe was everything they had hoped for.

Eventually they reached the foot of the towering French Alps and looked *straight up.* Their breath caught in their throats. To reach Italy they had to cross the mountains. Their map had proved to be a trustworthy guide so far, and their transportation had hummed along merrily as a new car should. They decided together to push on. They pointed the nose of the Volkswagon up and stepped on the gas.

Lori was driving that day. They rose swiftly and safely, and several hours later they were nearing the top when the road began to narrow. By then the view back down was breathtaking.

The narrowness of the road surprised them as the fair-sized highway dwindled to a small trail and finally became two faint tracks. Grass and weeds grew between the tracks, and judging from their undisturbed condition, the trail wasn't often used.

Mark voted to turn around. Lori was tempted, but they had come so far. Surely the road would broaden on the other side of the summit. She drove on.

The trail wound them through the middle of an unkempt yard surrounding a decrepit old farmhouse, the first sign of habitation they'd seen for miles. Chickens squawked and flapped their wings and pigs squealed as they raced out of sight underneath the ancient porch. It wasn't an inviting place to stop, even for a moment. Lori decided to go a little further.

Before long she realized her decision had been a mistake. Rounding a corner, they found themselves perched on a ledge barely wide enough to hold the car. Rough rocks scraped the paint from the door on her side, and Mark looked out of his window onto a dizzying drop of hundreds of feet.

Lori slammed her foot on the brake pedal and stopped. Now there was no room to turn around, and the prospect of backing even a few feet down that narrow ledge caused her heart to flutter uncontrollably.

Mark, with the absolute assurance of inexperience, said crisply, "Give me the wheel, Mother. I'll get us out of here!"

They changed places without leaving the car, because there was no room to stand on either side. Mark slipped the gears into reverse and cramped the wheel all the way to the left. He gunned the motor and whipped the little bug in a backwards circle at full speed. Miraculously they skimmed the cliff's edge without going over, but a resounding crash announced that the car's rear end and the mountain had tangled and the mountain had come up winner.

Their tailpipe was wedged tightly between two deeply embedded rocks, while the front bumper dangled over thin air. Front tires teetered on the last few inches of firm ground, threatening to slip over the edge at any moment. Lori's first thought was to wonder exactly how many miles they were from home.

Gingerly they eased their doors open, stepped out, and took

stock of the situation. No problem, Mark assured his anxious mother. He would simply dig the tailpipe out of the mountain with the handle of their new jack.

There is a universal, indisputable law—Murphy's law—that applies to situations like this and is dedicated to the proposition that if anything more *can* go wrong, it inevitably *will*. A search of the trunk revealed that the factory had goofed. The jack was there but its handle was missing. Now even Mark knew panic.

Sounds of running feet interrupted their uneasy thoughts as, huffing and puffing, two men and a woman panted their way around the bend. The older man came with a shovel slung over his shoulder.

Did they live in the broken-down farmhouse? Probably, but there was no telling for sure, since they spoke only French, while Lori and her son knew no French. They knew the area well, apparently, and had come prepared to help.

The woman was more agitated than Lori was, if possible. She threw her arms around Lori's neck and with much clucking and patting offered what consolation she could.

The older man moved at once to the car and ineffectually hacked at the mountainside with his shovel. The rocks were buried too deeply to be removed. Clearly that was not the answer to their dilemma.

Up to that point Lori had thought things were as bad as they could get. But then the younger man took action. He strode purposefully in their direction and with broad, expansive gestures let them know he wanted them back inside the car. Mark should steer while the man and his family pushed the car forward. They could tell his intentions without a common language, but they were not able to make him understand that his plan had one serious flaw: If the car moved forward, there was no place to go but straight down.

Lori peered over the edge of the cliff. She imagined she glimpsed their unidentified, bleached bones lying halfway down, drying in the summer sun. Surely the poor man must be demented. At the very least, he was determined.

Lori was familiar with the story of the biblical grain of mustard seed, the one that could move mountains, but she had never pictured her own faith being subject to the same test.

Never before had she uttered so fervent a prayer or packed so much solid conviction into so few seconds. There wasn't time to be flowery. As the man pressed toward them, all the spiritual power she possessed went from her in one silent scream for help.

Not ten seconds later they heard the pulse of an approaching engine. Around the same bend they had just traversed roared a big blue van carrying six men. Six husky men. The van screeched to a halt and the doors on both sides flew open. All six hurtled out.

The men were dressed in work clothes and appeared to be workers on their way to a construction job, perhaps unfamiliar with the territory and confused by the same map that had led the Hitchcocks astray.

They swooped down on the trapped automobile. With three on one side and three on the other, and as gracefully as if they were part of a choreographed dance routine, they bent, lifted, and pulled. In unison they freed the tiny car and turned it around to face the direction whence it had come. Without a glance at anyone and without a word they hurried to their van and in a flurry of dust and smoke disappeared down the road as mysteriously as they had come.

Lori and Mark were stunned. This was a solid, real-life answer to Lori's prayer for help, but they had no notion of where the men hailed from or what language they would have spoken *had* they spoken. And the Hitchcocks didn't stick around to try to figure it out. They jumped in their own car, and before the last vestiges of dust from the van had settled to the ground, they were gone.

Lori can laugh now as she recounts the experience, but behind her shaky laughter lies profound gratitude. She learned something valuable that day: Faith put to the ultimate test is a force to be reckoned with.

It may not have been the mountain that moved, but it was close enough.

$\mathscr{A}$ Lesson in Faith

ELAINE CANNON

Scott parked the car in the driveway closer to the street than the house. There were toys and equipment strewn up ahead. It had been a busy day for the "troops," as he referred to his family of three sons. There was a baby girl in their family, too, but she was still a harmless babe in arms. His annoyance was softened toward the children when he noticed the "replica helmet" Jason had begged for to wear on his Big Wheel so he'd feel as grown up as the bigger boys. Scott couldn't stay burned by boys' antics for long when the Lord had given him such fine ones.

Scott honked the car horn a couple of times, but no one rushed to move the toys so he could pull into the garage. That was a rule to which little attention was given, obviously. Rather than disturb the neighbors with his honking, he turned off the motor and gathered his day-planner to go inside the house. He would roust them out to move their play gear and put the car away later.

Scott loved being a father. Primarily that was because his own father had loved being a father, as he constantly declared in word and deed. Pop had advised Scott when the first baby came that the years went far too fast, so he had better make the most of fatherhood while influence over his children was still possible. *Influence?* thought Scott. *I haven't even been able to get them to put their stuff away at the end of play.*

Inside there was trauma, and Will raced to meet him when he shut the front door. The boy was crying and tugged on his pant leg to direct him toward the master bedroom. There was a scene to break any father's heart. Toddler Jason was flat on the bed, white and still. Mom sat beside him, gently rubbing her hand across his chest. Baby Lily, who obviously had been hurriedly plopped on the big bed, kicked and screamed. Everybody else shouted in anxiety over Jason. "Dad! Is Jason dead?" "Dad, save Jason!" "Jason can't breathe, Dad! Save him, save him." "We've called 911," his wife interjected, "but what if he dies first? He fell backwards from the Big Wheel and he isn't breathing." Then there was a chorus of, "Pray over him, Dad."

Scott ran to the top of the medicine cabinet and took the consecrated oil from its special box. Without really knowing any details of the problem, he asked the boys to fold their arms for prayer. He directed his weeping wife to kneel down beside the bed. He put his hands on the ailing boy's head, but for a few moments he couldn't speak. His thoughts raced. Jason threatened? Lose Jason? Could he demand of God that Jason rise and walk? Scott silently, fervently cried out to heaven for faith instead of fear as he performed the ritual of a father's blessing for Heavenly Father's spirit child. In moments his spirit calmed and he felt the warm confirmation surge through his body as he blessed Jason to awaken and be healed, by the power of the holy priesthood of God vested in him. He had battled with even saying the words "Thy will be done" before he closed the blessing, but then he knew his prayer had been heard. There was a murmured "Amen!" from Jason as Scott lifted his hands from his injured son's head. He felt a new lump well up in his own chest to see his little sons still in the reverent mood of prayer with their arms folded, their eyes scrunched shut. Of course Heavenly Father couldn't resist such pleadings from such devoted boys.

Suddenly Scott knelt down next to his wife beside the bed and guided the boys to do the same. Again he addressed Heavenly Father in prayer. This time he spoke as a father of a family grateful beyond expression to *be* a family, grateful for abundant blessings including trust in a loving Heavenly Father. Especially, they took time for a formal thanks to God for rousing Jason. *If I feel as I do about Jason,* thought Scott, *how much more must a good and perfect being like God love him!* All would be well, and the faith of the kneeling brothers would not be destroyed. They'd finally learn about putting toys away, but through a lesson in faith like this immediate answer to prayer, they would be helped along the road toward being loving fathers themselves.

Mary Fielding Smith and the Journey West

GARRETT H. GARFF

Sister Smith, I would advise you to give this up," the captain of the wagon company said, shaking his head. "Your outfit is not in any condition to make the journey west. You'd best go back to Winter Quarters and wait for some help. If you go with us you'll just be a burden on everyone else."

The words stung. Mary Fielding Smith—who had become a widow some four years before when her husband, Hyrum, and the Prophet Joseph were killed—did not want to be a burden. With the only means available to her, she had done her best to get together some wagons, teams, and supplies. She only wanted to do what the Church leaders counseled: gather to the Saints' new home in the valley of the Great Salt Lake. Now, despite all she had done to get ready, this man wanted her to give up just as the journey was really beginning.

She did not lash out. She did not break down. Her strength and her dignity would not allow that. Instead she calmly said: "Captain, I tell you now that not only will my family go west with this company, but we will arrive there before you do. And we won't ask for any help at all."

And thus in the late spring of 1848, Mary and the eight others, mostly children, for whom she was responsible pressed on for the Salt Lake Valley. It was a journey of about one thousand miles, and when all was said and done, it was Mary's faith in the Lord and his promises that sustained her and those in her care.

Mary demonstrated this faith in an especially powerful way

during the latter part of the trek. One of the oxen pulling Mary's wagons suddenly gave out and lay down on the ground. As people gathered around to see what had happened, it was thought that the ox was dying. To lose the animal would make it very difficult for Mary to go on.

The captain, impatient as always with the widow and her situation, strode up, looked at the ox, and then turned to Mary. "There," he growled, "I told you you would have to be helped and that you would be a burden on the company."

Mary made no reply. She went to one of her wagons, withdrew a bottle of consecrated oil, and handed the bottle to her brother Joseph, who was also traveling with the company. "Please, Joseph," she said, "will you administer to this animal? I have great need of him. The Lord knows that, and I have faith that he will honor your blessing."

Joseph Fielding and another priesthood holder poured the oil on the ox's head, laid their hands on the animal, and pronounced a blessing. To the amazement of the onlookers the ox got up and was soon pulling on the wagon as before. It was as if the animal had never been unwell.

As the company continued on the trail, two more of Mary's oxen who were failing were given blessings, and each time the results were the same: the animals were made whole.

Finally, though the journey certainly had not been easy, on September 23, 1848, Mary and her family arrived in the valley of the Great Salt Lake—one day ahead of the pessimistic captain from whom Mary, as promised, had never asked any help.

Thy Ways

SUSAN EVANS McCLOUD

I am coming now to know Thee,
Now at last. And trust Thee
Far beyond the hand of flesh.
At last my longings lift,
And I desire Thy blessings
Far above my worldly store.
I want to walk Thy ways with Thee,
And more—I want my spirit
To transcend, to soar.

Marriage
and
Family

The Panty Hose Problem

ELAINE CANNON

I know of a father who, for his daughter, would willingly drop his own life for the moment in order to crisis-shop the hosiery section of a department store.

The facts:

The father (Mike) was a young doctor and a member of a stake presidency—a very busy man. But he looked at his Emily and thought, *Love you!*

The mother was away at an important meeting. She left her daughter looking great in a new dress with new black designer panty hose to complete the outfit.

The daughter was hysterical. Mother was gone. Dad was home, but well—what did he know about such things as snagging and running the panty hose just minutes before the date is due at the door!

Emily was right. Dad didn't really know about such things, but he would try in the name of love.

He raced to the store and was baffled by the wide selection— *Black, yes! But what size, type? Queen—she's a queen to me. Support? She has mine. Tummy control? Good grief, what will women think of next!* Finally he just bought one of each. Better safe than a ruined evening.

$\mathscr{A}$ Son Brings His Family into the Church

BARBARA B. SMITH

I went to England longing to learn of the diversity and commonality of the Church in the lives of the women there. I found them as I asked the sisters to share their conversion stories with me. One Relief Society president told me that it was because of her son that she had joined the Church. I asked for the details and was very touched by the story.

She had been baking a cake when the doorbell rang. She went to the door and found two young men who wanted to tell her about the gospel. Knowing she had a cake baking in the oven, she thought if she could stall them long enough, the oven-timer bell would ring and the missionaries would know that she must go. That happened and she all but closed the door on them on her way to the kitchen. When she returned she was triumphant because the missionaries were no longer in sight. But as she shut the door and turned around, her little son called, "Mum, they're in here. I invited them to come into my room."

She then felt obligated to listen. She loved what she heard. She had them come back and share their message with her husband. They joined the Church and, in due time, went to the temple, sealing their little son to them. The mother was pregnant at the time, and when the baby was born her older son asked, "When are we going to take little brother to the temple and have him sealed to us?"

The mother's proud response was, "We don't have to take him because he was born in the covenant."

Her son began to cry. "That must mean he was more faithful in the world before this than I was, doesn't it?"

"Oh, no, my little son," she told him. "You must have been very faithful because, if it hadn't been for you, none of us would have had the gospel of Jesus Christ." She put her arms around him and loved him tenderly.

For Lack of Love
and Attention

JANENE WOLSEY BAADSGAARD

As I looked at my beautiful six-month-old baby, it seemed as if he had gone from a tiny, newborn infant to a wiggly, bubble-blowing baby without my even noticing. I longed for the hours I had had with my first child. I wanted those hours to rock and cuddle and fall asleep together. I wanted those hours for one-to-one sharing.

I wondered about our decision to have our children while we were young and raise them close together. As I folded the diapers, I watched my baby on the floor as he grabbed at his toes and tried to stuff them in his mouth. I knew it would only seem like moments before he would be crawling and then running and screaming with his brothers and sisters. I wondered if my baby would suffer from lack of individual time and attention.

Just then my two-year-old son ran into the room. As soon as he saw his little brother, he ran toward him, lay his head on his back, and patted his bottom. Then he jumped up, ran and grabbed his favorite tattered blanket, and covered him gently.

Then my three-year-old daughter came into the room. When she saw her little brother on the floor, she immediately lay down next to him. The baby turned his face to her and smiled and cooed as she smothered his face with kisses and said, "Oh, you cute little button. I love you. You're my favorite buddy."

Then my seven-year-old daughter came into the room and sat the baby up on the blanket. She lifted him to his feet and they rubbed noses.

Then my five-year-old son came into the room and said, "Hey, it's my turn to play with Jacob. You always hog up too much time."

Then my eight-year-old daughter walked into the room and promised she'd do the seven-year-old's dinner dishes if she let her rock Jacob. She picked up the baby and carried him to the oversized rocker.

The two-year-old ran and grabbed the baby's pacifier and popped it into his mouth while the rest of them snuggled together on the rocker. My five-year-old spread his blanket over everyone's knees after he crawled to the chair to join the others.

My seven-year-old picked up a book and started to read to a quiet audience. "Once upon a time," she began.

That baby is suffering from lack of attention and love? I thought as I finished folding the last diaper and headed toward the kitchen sink to do a pile of dishes.

Slowly my self-doubts melted as I watched my children together in the rocker they had so appropriately named our "love seat."

ℒarge Family

KATHLEEN "CASEY" NULL

Latter-day Saint families generally have more than the average amount of children, which makes them unusual.

One unusual thing about large families is experience. They have experiences no small family could imagine. It's an entire dimension.

Having a large family means that you can double your efforts. You can be up in the wee hours pacing the floor with a baby and waiting for a teenager to come home at the same time.

Having a large family means never suffering from loneliness . . . even when you think you'd enjoy the experience.

Having a large family means two hours and two carts to get through the supermarket.

Having a large family means having your own pew in the chapel.

Having a large family means having a clothing inventory that rivals that of a major clothing chain.

Having a large family means having older children who can take younger ones for innumerable bathroom visits during sacrament meeting.

Having a large family means always having indigestion after having to talk with your mouth full, eating while getting things from the kitchen, stopping fights, and getting up and down to put overturned glasses upright.

Having a large family means never again will you enjoy the luxury of a low profile as your offspring reach out into the world to embarrass, disgrace, and glorify.

Having a large family means never a dull sacrament meeting.

Having a large family means plenty of opportunities to learn patience, discipline, management, love, forgiveness, and how much effort it really takes to become a forever family.

Another Baby?

LINDA J. EYRE

The Reservation

I could feel it coming on. The baby was getting around on his own pretty well, and I felt wonderful. The other four children, although they had their individual ups and downs, were basically secure and happy. The piano practicing was getting more regular because I was able to be behind it a little more consistently. And with the baby just beginning to walk, I felt wings of independence and a sense of joy in watching the children grow and relate to the world around them. What worried me was the nagging feeling in the back of my mind that it might be time to have another baby.

I quickly remembered the many times I had said to myself when the last baby was tiny, "Now, remember, remember, *remember* how hard it is to have a new little baby! It takes all your time and attention. You never get enough sleep because you're up twice in the night with the baby, and then of course there's no hope for a nap during the day with a two-year-old and a four-year-old in the house, both ready to 'search and destroy' at any moment. You're so tired that you're a grouch with your husband and children all the time. Besides, you have to be on duty every three or four hours—day and night—to nurse the baby, so that every outing, whether it be a fireside or grocery shopping, has to be scheduled to the minute.

"Waking every morning to the baby's cries cuts down on and sometimes eliminates your time with the scriptures and makes it much harder to have morning prayer. And it's like a never-ending race every morning to change and feed the baby while you supervise the practicing and settle an argument about who gets to sit by Daddy, before you organize the breakfast amidst pleas of 'Write my teacher a note' and 'Give me some lunch money.' Then you get to dress and then dress again the two-year-old who has been using the butter for play dough while you check to see that the beds are made and oversee the getting ready for school, complete with the perpetual last-minute scramble for Saren's toothbrush, Shawni's mittens, and Josh's shoes. Finally you struggle to get them out of the door with a smile pasted over your gritted teeth and a 'Have a nice day.' Next you try to help Saydi get her shirt on frontwards for nursery school while talking on the phone to someone with a problem, and then you have to fish the cat out of the toilet where Saydi has put him to try his luck.

"You just don't have time for another baby!" I told myself over and over, to help me remember how lovely the comparative peace of routine was becoming.

We, as a family, were just going into the third year of the greatest opportunity of our lives. My husband was president of the London South Mission, and we were having a marvelous experience—not without challenges, however, as the demands were great. Feeding mobs of missionaries, speaking at conferences, preparing our home for firesides for investigators and for new members who were struggling, and fixing dinners for everyone from stake presidents to General Authorities to members of Parliament kept me hopping.

Always before I had been thoroughly excited about the prospect of having a new spirit join our family. We had been married eight years and had five children: Saren, seven; Shawni, six; Josh, four; and Saydi, two and one-half, had come with us from America, and we had been blessed to have one child born in England—our little British boy, Jonah. My hesitation this time caused me to examine my own heart. Was I afraid after Jonah's difficult arrival? That was not it. Could it be that I simply did not want to give up my freedom to participate in all the activities of the mission? As I wrestled with the pros and cons (mostly cons) and with the deep, dark feeling I got every time I thought about another baby, my husband, who was feeling the same dilemma, suggested that on Sunday we should follow the same procedure that we had with the other children and have a special day of fasting and prayer to get an answer.

To be very honest, I did not even want to ask, because I was afraid of what the answer might be. However, I finally consented, with the thought in mind that maybe the answer this time *might* be, "No, not yet, take care of the responsibilities you have now and wait." *Oh, please tell me that!* I thought.

"Okay, Richard," I said in my most determined voice. "But we have *got* to have a very explicit answer and we'll have to fast forty-eight or even seventy-two hours, if necessary, to be absolutely sure." I saw him go a little pale around the mouth, because fasting is one of his hardest things. After a minute he patted me on the shoulder and said, "Let's start with twenty-four and see how it goes."

Sunday rolled around, and as we neared the end of our fast we compared our lists of pros and cons and started talking about them in earnest so that we could take a yes or no decision to the Lord for confirmation. About that time, however, the children began to get pretty noisy. Daddy called Saren, our oldest, over to the table.

"Would you please take your brothers and sisters up to the playroom and entertain them for an hour while Mom and Dad have a very serious talk, honey?" Curious about what we were doing, our very mature little seven-year-old demanded to know what was so important before she would consent.

"Well," he said after a moment of deliberation, "we're trying to decide whether or not to ask Heavenly Father to send a new little person to be in our family." She smiled wryly and happily herded the others up the stairs.

For what seemed like a very long time we worked on an extensive list of possibilities, and finally decided mutually, much to my chagrin, that it was time to have another baby if we could get a confirmation from the Lord and if he would grant us that privilege once again. As we knelt down, I remember having felt what I can only describe as black, dark, and numb. I just didn't know how I could possibly do it! I suppose I was hoping not for a confirmation but for a "stupor of thought" that would tell us to reconsider.

The Revelation

Kneeling across from me and holding my hands, Richard began the prayer. The minute he said, "We have decided that now is the time to ask for another choice spirit, if that is thy will for us," I began to feel what I would describe as a bright light of peace settling over me, starting from the top of my head and spreading to every part, right down to my fingers and toes. It was as though the Lord was saying forcefully, in his own peaceful way: "It's all right, Linda. This baby is what you need; I've got a good one up here—one who needs to come now and who will teach you many things. I'll provide a way to get it all done. All is well. Be at peace."

By the time Richard's prayer was finished and I had offered mine, a conviction that a new person would join us and that all would be well was burning inside me, overwhelming, all-consuming, and undeniable. I was a new person, at perfect peace and ready for change. Most answers the Lord had given me were not nearly so dramatic—merely nudges in the right direction and good feelings. I was so gratified for this special, sure knowledge that he was there, loving and caring and answering.

While we were still holding hands and glowing in the aftermath of this beautiful spiritual experience, Saren, who could somehow sense that we were finished, came trotting into the dining room with a happy smile on her face and some pieces of paper in her hand.

"I organized the kids upstairs," she said. "I had them all sit in a circle on the floor and gave them each a piece of paper. Shawni and I wrote the names of the kids at the top of each paper. We told them to put a big check in the middle of the paper if they wanted a new baby brother or sister." She handed me five pieces of paper with five bold checkmarks below the names. It was now a unanimous family decision!

In the following few days, largely because of the good feelings I had about the answer the Lord had given me, I felt particularly close to him and my mind was flooded with things that were revelations to me. I had been going along these past seven years being a faithful, loving mother: having children, learning the hows and whens and wheres, but not really realizing the *whys!*

I projected myself ahead in time and tried to look at life and the childbearing years from an eternal perspective. I was startled to realize that in all eternity I would have only about twenty years in which to bear physical children on a physical earth and reap the eternal joys therein: the joy of learning to manage time and feelings and people, and the joy of molding lives and developing relationships that would help me to learn and grow forever. Only twenty years! Right now it seems like such a long time to change diapers and stand in foyers with fussy, noisy children, to prepare meals and put on bandages. Yet (as so many mothers just past the childbearing years tell me), soon there will be only a memory of how I did, to what extent I was anxiously engaged in grasping all the joy and happiness that was there for me to find in that short time. Then it will be over—forever!

I began to concentrate less on the difficulties of pregnancy and childbearing, on the complications of organizing life around an infant, on the heavy responsibility of having another person totally dependent on me. I began to see it all from a new perspective: My eyes were opened, and like a warm, wooly parachute settling over me, the whys began to make themselves manifest.

Having another child is a great blessing to be looked forward to with enthusiasm and excitement. I began to relish the change (the essence of the Savior's message: "You can change") and the challenges that would follow, to pour my energies into this real priority and to organize my life to do so, because the opportunity for that particular time in life only comes once and doesn't last very long. Children grow and change; so do situations; so do I. I began to relish the joy of balancing my life to make scrubbing floors and windows secondary to watching and relating to children and perceiving their needs before they became real problems.

I began to realize what a great blessing it is to struggle to teach a child the correct principles of life, and to make the home a great medium to do so. What we teach our children, how we mold their characters to try to make them responsible family members, loyal citizens, and noble children of God, affects not only us and them but their children and their children's children—an awesome and exciting challenge!

As the days passed I began to realize that my body was my most valuable earthly possession because of the miracles it could perform. If the condition that it was in was the determining factor in how many children I'd be privileged to have, I'd better take it a little more seriously. I felt an urgency to get in first-class physical condition so that I would be *able* to bear children as well as humanly possible for me. I decided that being in shape would alleviate the discomfort of the first few and last few months of the pregnancy, not to mention the benefits to the health of the baby. I had always known it made a difference, but I hadn't taken it seriously enough in the past to worry much about it. By "number six" with the hopes of more to come, it was serious business. I began a short crash course of physical fitness and realized that keeping fit between pregnancies was as important as during. The whole revelation was exhilarating.

The things that had worried me during past pregnancies seemed small and unimportant in light of the eternal perspective. Suddenly all the counsel given by the prophets came to life: "Have children unless there are health reasons involved. Put your family first; cut out the trivia, the excess, and concentrate on *them*. The rewards will be immediate *and* long-term . . . forever."

Postscript: The Resolution, February 6, 1999

As the baby in this story, our son Talmadge, is now a wonderful ambassador for the Lord in the Brazil Campinas Mission and is turning twenty on this very day, I decided that a postscript to this story might be enlightening. That seven-pound-two-ounce baby boy is now six-feet-nine-inches tall and wears a size 15 shoe. Since the day he burst into the harsh lights of that delivery room in Epsom, Surrey, England, exactly twenty years ago, calmly sucking on the knuckle of his index finger, he has been the personification of and a continual confirmation of the answer to our prayer. Looking into his eyes those first moments of his earthly existence was almost scary. In those deep, dark eyes, I saw a remarkable spirit, fresh from Heavenly Father.

Of course, all of our children—who were also fasted and prayed for—have their own wonderful stories complete with joys and sorrows, but Talmadge was, without contest, the easiest, most contented baby we ever had. He sucked on that knuckle through long meetings with General Authorities, many of which lasted hours past feeding time, and he endured many a cold bath in the sinks of church restrooms while we were holding zone and district meetings. As he grew, he even sat quietly in the grocery cart as massive piles of missionary munchies were stacked around him.

In elementary school, this great young man struggled with difficult learning disabilities. However, through dogged diligence and perseverance over the years, he somehow learned to make his artistic, creative way of right-brained thinking fit into the meticulously calculative left-brained system we all live in well enough to be able to enter Brigham Young University last year. Both his achievements and his insights never cease to amaze us.

There was no way I could have known those many years ago the joy this child would bring to our family, but I'm here to tell you that answers to prayers are real! More than twenty years since we knelt that night in apprehensive prayer, the profound words we received from our Heavenly Father still flash in my mind: "It's all right, Linda. This baby is what you need; I've got a good one up here—one who needs to come now and who will teach you many things. I'll provide a way to get it all done. All is well. Be at Peace."

Family Home Evenings
in Your Little House

GEORGE DURRANT

With trembling fingers, I gripped the eight-page script I had written during the previous week. It was my best effort, but would it be good enough to satisfy the other eight members of the Family Home Evening Writing Committee?

I began to read.

The first three pages discussed how, in 1963, President Harold B. Lee had re-emphasized the need for families to have a weekly family home evening. I noticed Sister Hale, our leader, nod her approval at the direction I was taking. Grant Hardy, perhaps the most astute member of our committee, moved forward, then backward in his chair. The other six members sat motionless.

I read on, describing experiences I had heard others report regarding their family home evenings.

Soon I came to the page where I had expressed my feelings of what had happened with Marilyn and me and our children.

I was not prepared for what happened next. From the sixth page of the script, I read about asking my children if they could tell me of a personal experience of a prayer being answered. Seven-year-old Kathryn replied, "Last week when the garbage truck came, one of the garbage men had a big bandage on his hand. I prayed that his hand would get better. Today when he came, the bandage was gone."

I felt considerable emotion as I read that simple story aloud. I paused, but then I was able to carry on.

Next I read:

"We sat in our front room using the manual. The lesson we were discussing centered on saying good things about each other. One by one, each child was the target, and all the rest of us took turns saying good things about that child.

"A beautiful spirit came into the room.

"Finally, it was Marilyn's turn to be the one. Each child quickly stated something good about her. Finally it was our ten-year-old son Matt's turn to speak.

"He softly said, 'Dad, if I said all the good things that I know about Mom, we'd be here all night.'"

Having read these words, a feeling of love and gratitude came into my heart so forcefully that I could hardly continue to read.

After pausing long enough to take a deep breath, I read, "Oh, my dear son, I feel the same way about her. I love her with all my heart."

Having said this, a flood of dear feelings for my family and for the joy of family home evening came into my soul.

I could read no more. I began to gently sob.

My kind associates spoke tender words of comfort, even though my sobs had become contagious and they too were in tears.

Finally, after a minute or so, I gathered myself together and read the conclusion of the script.

The script was never used, but that didn't matter, because through writing and reading it, I had a spiritual witness that having family home evenings can result in sacred blessings that can be a major force in uniting a family forever.

I'll Bet You Don't Know What Day This Is

BROOKIE PETERSON

One morning a woman said to her husband as he was leaving for work, "I'll bet you don't know what day this is."

"Of course I know what day this is," he replied resentfully. And with that he left for the office.

Later that morning a knock came at the door, and the woman was delighted to find that it was a delivery for her—a dozen red roses. A big box of gourmet chocolates arrived in the afternoon, and towards evening the local jewelry store delivered a beautiful pearl necklace.

Excitedly the woman awaited her husband's return home. When he finally arrived she hugged him and exclaimed, "Oh, sweetheart, first the roses, then the chocolates, and then the necklace—I can't remember when I have had such a perfectly wonderful Groundhog Day!"

*B*oys

KATHLEEN "CASEY" NULL

D_o you know what it means to have three or more sons?" asked Sister Evans.

What is this, I thought, a trick question?

Sister Evans, experienced grandmother, has just spent nearly two hours sitting on the pew behind me. She couldn't have helped but notice that I have three sons, and a daughter who can hold her own.

"It means"—I decided to give it a try—"going through ten pounds of peanut butter a week."

"Yes, I know, but what else?" Her eyes were lit up with amusement.

"It means . . . always having grimy switchplates."

She smiled. "Well, granted, but what else?"

"It means learning to co-exist peacefully with a managerie of rats, birds, dogs, rabbits, fish, caterpillars, frogs, worms, and sow bugs."

"Oh . . ." she rolled her eyes in mock disgust, "I nearly forgot about that. But that's not quite it."

"OK. It means buying a year's supply of tube socks every other month and having two sons per morning wail, 'I can't find any socks!'"

"Yes, I remember," she sighed, "The socks probably got up and walked away. But that's not it."

"Then it means living in a locker room atmosphere."

"Of course," she said. "But that's still not *it*."

"Then how about having three or more sons means never

having to say, 'Help yourselves to seconds . . . there's plenty, you really should eat more.' "

"Well . . ." she sighed.

"Wait, I know, I'm probably just guessing at the wrong level. How about this? It means running a workshop to teach boys to deal with life when they go on missions and leave the nest."

"You're getting a little closer," she said impatiently.

"It means, preparing boys to hold the priesthood?"

"Is that a statement or a question?"

She didn't wait for my reply. "I'll tell you what it means. Being the parent of three or more sons means you can rest assured. If you can raise these boys you won't need to be tested any further."

Sounds fair to me.

The Little Rescuer

ELAINE L. JACK

I have a good friend who told me of a personal rescue that she holds close to her heart. She was a college student. It was near the end of her senior year, and things were not falling together as she had hoped. She had applied to graduate school but wasn't sure about taking that next step in her education. She was very involved in student affairs and recognized that these experiences that she loved were coming to an end. She was dating the missionary for whom she'd waited for two years, but she was also dating his best friend and had been for most of the time the missionary was gone. At that moment, her journey was a nightmare.

It was a Friday afternoon, and she was particularly down-hearted. She hadn't heard from any graduate schools. She was juggling dates for the weekend with both men. She had papers to write and projects to finish. Her little ten-year-old brother was the only one home, and he was begging her to play a game with him. She couldn't stand to deal with life, so she left. She walked out the front door and up the street, and then she turned and began to walk toward the freeway. As she walked she heard a crunch on the gravel behind her, and turning she saw her little brother. He looked at her face streaked with tears and then asked, "Where ya going?"

She replied in a voice most dramatic, "I don't know."

For a minute he looked at her, not sure what to do, and then he said, "Do you want to go to Skaggs?"

He was a rescuer that day. A little ten-year-old chasing a lost-looking sister around the corner and up the street. He knew something was wrong, didn't know what, and yet he was the only one there. He made her laugh, and they went to Skaggs. She'll never forget that day he saved her. He more than made her day.

How long has it been since you've made someone's day? Or made a very bad day just a little bit better? Sometimes climbing up on that white horse feels good for the rider as well as the one in distress.

$\mathcal{K}$idding Around in Your Little House

GEORGE DURRANT

After my teaching day is done, I walk down the hill past BYU's Smith Fieldhouse. My heart feels the sort of pure happiness that is so often the lot of someone who loves his work. Soon I cross University Avenue and walk the final three blocks home. My pace quickens as I turn the last corner and have just over one hundred yards to go. My heart pounds with excitement as, in my mind, I already can see Marilyn standing with her nose pressed against the window, looking out to catch the first glimpse of her handsome, homecoming husband.

Now, if you know Marilyn, you are already laughing at what I just wrote. And when Marilyn reads the above, she will in jest agree, "Oh yeah, I can hardly do anything all day long except wait for him to return."

Somehow my semi-sincere statements and Marilyn's gentle counterattacks are the spice that makes me look forward each night to coming home. The children are all married now, except Mark, and he is on a mission. Whereas for years I came home to a throng of excited children, now I come home to just Marilyn. Why is it that coming home is even sweeter now than ever before?

There are, of course, many reasons. But one important one is that Marilyn and I like to kid around and have fun. Now, don't get me wrong. Often I am far too sober when we are together, but sometimes I wish you could see me. I come home and I'm really funny. Well, at least sort of funny. And when I am, Marilyn is funny back, and when we are funny like that we sense and often say things that let us know that we are deeply in love.

I don't know what it is about kidding around and laughing that makes it so much easier to have love flare up in your heart. But it seems to me that having fun without having to do fun things creates a feeling that is to love what rich fertile soil is to a tender plant.

I wish sometimes I was funnier and that Marilyn was too. Often we don't seem to be in a fun mood, and so we just sit and act like duds—at least I do.

Maybe that's all right; maybe much of life is best lived as a dud. But I'm sure glad that quite often we rise up and have some homemade kidding around.

Here is an example of some pure fun. We've had dinner and Marilyn is about to leave for her calligraphy class. (To me, she is the best calligrapher in Utah and even up as far as Idaho.) I gently say, "Marilyn, don't be goofing off in your calligraphy class. You are not there to have fun—but to work."

She quickly replies, "Working is fun when you're a calligrapher." Then, because I'm a water colorist, she says, "It's you water color people who never have any fun."

I reply, "That is because water color is tough to do. It's not easy like calligraphy."

By then she's out of the door, and I'm chuckling to myself about my victory. As I press my nose against the window and watch her go, I say to myself, "I miss her already, and she isn't even out of the driveway."

I called the above "victory," but it has been some thirty plus years since I won or even desired to win a battle of wits with Marilyn. She always wins, but I constantly award myself the sportsmanship trophy because I am so goodnatured about my losses to her. And when she makes her supposedly funny remarks, I don't ever laugh, because that would cause her to think that she is clever. Sometimes, however, I find myself thinking, "She really is funny." Then I realize again that the way she says funny things about me makes me know how much she adores me.

I recall a conversation we had after I returned from my mission. I was telling her a rather serious story of some of my high school frustrations—things such as my not being a star athlete, or popular, or a student-body leader. Suddenly she was holding her left hand in front of her with her thumb and forefinger about two inches apart. At the same time she was moving her right hand back and forth near the left hand. Simultaneously she was humming a rather high pitch. I stopped and said, "What are you doing?"

She replied, "I'm playing the world's smallest violin to accompany the world's saddest story."

I felt like bursting out in laughter, but all I could do was say, "Very funny." I grabbed her hand and said, "You'd never get away with such antics if I didn't love you so much." And, oh, how I did and still do love such futile efforts on her part to be funny!

People who know both Marilyn and me think I'm funny and Marilyn is sober. Not so. Within the walls of our home and our love, she is the funny one. And as I write that, I chuckle to myself and feel so grateful to have a funny wife—a funny friend.

I could go on and on about her humor, but she'd read it and become prideful. So I'll leave it there for now.

In our home through the years, my children, who can't seem to tell a quality sense of humor from an average one, have chosen to use their laughs more frequently in support of their mother's remarks than mine.

When she tells them of my inability to dance, they laugh. Of course, that makes me feel bad. I tried to learn to dance in high school, but in those days you danced really close to the girl and that was too much for me. I took a social dance class in college and finally got an E. But I was better than that. It's just that I could never seem to get the beat.

Once, when Marilyn broke her foot, I thought I'd turn the tables on her, so one night, in front of the children, I said, "Marilyn, I've been thinking I'd like to go dancing. Should we go tonight?" I felt quite clever in my remarks, but she replied, "I don't want to have you break my other foot."

The children, who couldn't see the humor in my remarks, roared with laughter at hers, and all that did was encourage her and make her laugh at her own supposed joke. Inside, I was beside myself with the happy feelings of such fun. But I just protested, "Way to go, children, laugh all you want. But just remember you are laughing at someone who loves you more than can ever be said." They looked at me, and Marilyn did too, with that wonderful look of complete love.

It's as I said earlier. Growing right out of the soil of kidding around come feelings of love that somehow in such moments can be expressed with surprising power.

What Can I Be?

PATRICIA T. HOLLAND

When my daughter, Mary, was just a small child, she was asked to perform for a PTA talent contest. This is her experience exactly as she wrote it in her seven-year-old script.

"I was practicing the piano one day, and it made me cry because it was so bad. Then I decided to practice ballet, and it made me cry more; it was bad, too. So then I decided to draw a picture because I knew I could do that good, but it was horrid. Of course it made me cry.

"Then my little three-year-old brother came up, and I said, 'Duffy, what *can* I be? What can *I* be? I can't be a piano player or an artist or a ballet girl. What can I be?' He came up to me and whispered, 'You can be my sister.'"

In an important moment, those five simple words changed the perspective and comforted the heart of a very anxious child. Life became better right on the spot, and as always, tomorrow was a brighter day.

Seeking the Spirit

Taking Down Fences

ARDETH G. KAPP

Inside fences, Ardie, invisible to others, are very real. They can sometimes hold us captive," Dad cautioned. "And furthermore, they are impossible to take down unless we ourselves determine to do it." Then, looking out again at our extended wealth, he seemed to be pondering as he added one more comment before changing the subject. "It's sometimes a hard job to take down a fence. It may take a lifetime."

As late afternoon approached, Dad pulled his watch from the little pocket in his overalls. "It's time to call it quits," he announced; and be began putting the tools in the back of the old blue truck. Sitting side by side, we bounced along over the ruts that had been left in the dirt road following the last rain storm. A cloud of dust trailed behind us as we headed down the three-mile stretch to our home.

"You're a good helper," he said; and I knew he really meant it. "We do good work together," he continued, "and today we learned a lot about fences." I wasn't sure what he meant. Now weary of fence building, I decided to leave the responsibility for that lesson to Dad. If it was important, I knew he would bring it up again.

It was nearing the end of the school year, almost a full season since our experience of fence building. For me it had been a long, hard winter—a season of harsh temperatures and many storms. It's true that the thermometer did not record such adversities, but I knew that the severity of any Canadian blizzard could never be more threatening to a human being than the devastation I had repeatedly experienced at school that year. I remember the occasion, following a weekly examination, when every student's name was written on the chalkboard in the hall for everyone to see. The names did not appear in alphabetical order, but in rank order—the highest at the top, the lowest in the most conspicuous place of all, the bottom. Even with my name in that horrifying spot, I felt a faint twinge of gratitude for the only two names that followed mine on the list (in spite of the fact that these two were German students who were struggling with the language).

One day after school as I stood at our kitchen window looking out on a world that seemed so destructive and cruel, I could hear my mother reaching for words that might help quiet the storm she knew was raging inside me. "But you must realize," she said, "that you've missed so much school. You've been ill and . . . and . . ." All her explanations made little difference to me when in my hand I had the evidence (my report card) to confirm my conviction that I was dumb and that the whole world, at least all my friends, knew it.

Dad called me into the living room, and I sat on the footstool in front of his big chair. Leaning forward, he spoke in an almost pleading tone. "I have a concern," he confessed.

"What is it, Dad?" I asked, fearing that his concern was for my report card.

Taking both my hands in his big hands and looking at me as if to see clear through me, without any explanation or elaboration, he simply said, "Before the last day of school, I want you to go to Mrs. Shane and express appreciation for all she has tried to teach you this year."

"But, Dad," I exploded, "don't you understand?"

He nodded and said, "I do."

And then like steam escaping from a valve under pressure, I began: "But Mrs. Shane hates me. She failed me. She hasn't been fair. She always asks me why I can't be like my brother. Dad, I can't." In a final cry of anguish I sobbed, "I hate her!"

Dad again just nodded, and with more feeling this time said, "I know you do."

We sat in silence for a long time. I struggled with the unbelievable request from my father who I thought loved me, while he searched our shared reservoir of experiences for just the right mortar to make his reasoning hold together. With a faraway look in his eye and with his ability to recreate in vivid detail our most treasured experiences together, he began, "Remember the time last fall when we were fence builders together?" That reminder was a partial relief to my troubled heart. I nodded. "And do you remember that we talked about inside fences and how hard it is to take them down?" That was the part I couldn't remember. I guess he thought that in this setting it had some application and he tried again.

He told me about how he understood my feelings and how he had watched me struggle with school and with my teacher, Mrs. Shane. "Now about the fence, Ardie," he explained, getting right to the point. "As you have struggled with your lessons and made considerable progress, I have been very proud of you; but I have also watched you gradually build a fence, one post at a time. A fence that should never have been built at all. It will limit you. It will keep you confined and hold you in and restrict your progress. It is an inside fence, Ardie, and only you can take it down and only if you want to."

How could he know all this? I had never complained at home about my teacher. I knew better than that. How did he know how I felt inside? His seriousness prompted me to ask the question he had hoped for. "But how can I do it, Dad?"

And then he went back to where he had started as he repeated: "Before the last day of school I want you to go to Mrs. Shane and express appreciation for all she has tried to teach you this year. You don't have to do it today or even tomorrow. There are ten days before the end of school, and a fence isn't put up or taken down in a day."

The remaining ten days were silently numbered without any prodding from Dad. One evening as a family everyone talked about hard things they had each done, fences they had taken down. Dad told us about a problem he had through a misunderstanding with a neighbor, and I learned for the first time why he secretly shoveled our neighbor's walk each morning after a snow storm before anyone else was up. I always thought he was just clearing the walk, but he explained that he was taking down a fence.

The next morning in our family prayer, my mom asked for special help for each of us. At that moment I thought I might be able to take down a fence, maybe even that day. I would see.

I sat all day in school as Mrs. Shane in her usual way tried to get the attention of the students by embarrassing them and shouting at them. "Priscilla," she said, "your voice is so loud you could stand on your porch and call all over town without a telephone." In the afternoon it was Harvey who was the victim of her wrath. "Harvey," she shouted from her desk in the center of the room, "if all your brains were put in a bullet there wouldn't be enough powder to blow your hat off." No, I couldn't take the fence down today, I thought, maybe tomorrow.

Somehow thinking about fences and the good day Dad and I had spent together building ours last fall eased the feelings inside for a moment at least. Dad was right. It's the inside fences we build ourselves that bind us. Maybe Mrs. Shane had lots of inside fences that kept her troubled and cross, I thought. I surely didn't want to be like that.

Finally the school bell rang. All the kids left immediately. They always did. No one stays to talk to a teacher they don't like. I fussed around my desk to purposely delay until, except for Mrs. Shane and me, the room was empty. Looking up from her desk and glancing over her glasses she said with a crisp voice, "Well?"

Without really seeing her (only anticipating my joy when I would see Mom and Dad after school that night), I hurried up the aisle to her desk. Standing with my head down, not looking at this teacher I had learned to fear and even hate, I blurted out my message that would, I hoped, take down the fence and no more. "Mrs. Shane," I said, my heart pounding against my chest, "I want to tell you thanks for trying to teach me, even if I didn't learn." With my message delivered I was free to run from that threatening position and, as I hoped, never have to talk to her again.

But before I could escape, she reached for my hand and drew me to her. She put her arm around my waist, but I felt myself pulling back. She waited a minute which seemed like an hour. "Thank you," she said in a quiet voice that didn't sound like my teacher's voice at all.

I glanced up to see her face. *Can this be Mrs. Shane?* I thought. She looked different, not so scary, more sad. Her eyes looked unhappy. She even sounded different. We visited a minute before I left. *Just three days before the end of school,* I thought, and now I wondered why I had never really seen her before.

I ran all the way home from the school, down the path, across the stile, through the open field by the church, past the gooseberry bushes in front of the Bucks' home, and past the Woods' white horse. Without slackening my pace, I licked two fingers on my right hand, stamped the palm of my left hand, and hit my left hand with my fist for good luck. I rounded the corner by the garage into our backyard where Dad was fixing a picket fence for the sweet peas to climb. Quite out of breath, I wondered how I would report my victory.

Dad had adjusted from his kneeling position to sit on the ground and with his arms outstretched and a big smile on his face he said: "Well, tell me about it, 'fence wrecker.' How was it?" We sat on the ground together while I caught my breath. He listened to all of the details, interrupting only to ask me occasionally just how I felt at a particular time; and then he would nod and continue to look at me over his heavy eyebrows.

Having heard the full report carefully recited, Dad, searching my eyes, questioned me, "And how do you feel about Mrs. Shane, my dear?"

"I don't hate her, Dad," I honestly confessed.

He smiled and nodded, "The rest will come."

Mom, We Need to Talk

EARLENE BLASER

One night my oldest was late coming home. He had gone out with his best friend and some girls whom they had met at the mall (can you imagine?). I hadn't a clue who the girls were or where the group had gone. I admit I had been spoiled because I had the luxury of knowing most of my children's friends. It wasn't a family rule or anything, I just enjoyed being with them. The hour was late enough that I had progressed straight through *mad* and was now at *worry*. I planned to let him have it with both guns when he got home. I had visions of him in sackcloth and ashes repenting while he endured his sentencing of being grounded for the rest of his teenage life. I vacillated between feeling scared and angry numerous times. All mothers of teenagers know exactly what I mean: after you see they are alive, you give a war whoop and tell the world that you are going to "kill 'em." The prayer that started in my heart turned full bloom on my knees as I pleaded that he was safe and that I would see him again. This sounds a little dramatic, but after all, it was my first experience with my first teenager. I then prayed that if and when he came home, I would know how to show him my love amidst all the anger. I wanted to do this just right. He walked in the door, quickly apologized for making me worry and losing the sleep he knew I desperately needed. Then he said, "Mom, we need to talk."

For the first time in my life that I remember, I didn't say a word. I sat and listened. He told me how grateful he was for his friends and their standards, how he loved his high school, even what a great influence Principal Hawkins was on his life. The evening had been spent talking, and they lost track of time. (Has this ever happened to me?) These girls shared how they felt great pressure to abandon their personal standards. They didn't understand how to have a good time without breaking God's laws and commandments. He expressed his love to me for his family and his best friend, Shane. Then he mumbled, "I'm tired; I'm going to bed."

Like many significant moments in motherhood, this night is lost to my son's memory, but I will never forget it. It was very much against my nature to handle the situation as I did. I had asked for help and for once was smart enough to listen to the answer. I never did know who the girls were, but I was so grateful that through my patience I got to know my son better. Without jumping to conclusions about his irresponsibility and being inconsiderate, I was able to listen to his spirit. I felt wise. He was the teacher and I had been taught.

$\mathcal{I}$t's My Baby!

BARBARA B. SMITH

$\mathbf{D}$orothy, David, and their new little baby son had barely lived long enough in a California ward to have visiting teachers assigned. Two sisters were driving down the freeway on a Saturday morning, going to a year-end sale, when suddenly the one who was driving said, "I feel impressed that we should go and visit that sister who just moved into our ward, the new one assigned to our district."

Her companion objected, "No one goes to visit a new woman in the ward this early on a Saturday morning. But if you feel that we should go, let's go to the sale and then stop by there on the way home." The driver of the car didn't say much more, but when they came to the off-ramp, she turned the car onto it and said, "I just feel that we must go now. I hope you don't mind too much."

When she stopped the car in front of the home the companion said, "Are you certain you feel we need to go in now?"

"Yes, I really do," she answered. They got out of the car, walked up the pathway to the door, and rang the bell. Dorothy came to the door with her baby in her arms.

They began, "We are your visiting teachers." That was all they got to say before Dorothy started to cry. "Is something wrong?" they asked.

"Yes," she said, "it's my baby! Every time I put him down he seems to stop breathing, and so I have held him all night long and prayed that someone would come to help me."

"Why didn't you take him to the hospital or call a doctor?" they asked.

"As you know, we're new here. My husband is out of town on business, so I don't have a car to get to the hospital, and I don't know anyone to call to help me."

The visiting teachers were anxious to help and the mother was deeply grateful. As quickly as they could, they drove the mother and baby to the hospital. At the emergency entrance a doctor took the baby, and worked with him for quite some time. When he came back he said, "You are very fortunate to have gotten this child here when you did. He could not have lived but a little while longer." That baby is now a grown man and a strong advocate for the Church. The Lord had a work for him to do, as well as an important work for those visiting teachers. They were a fine example of how responsive visiting teachers can be instruments of the Lord in filling critical assignments in cases of real need.

$\mathscr{T}$he White Handkerchief

MARILYNNE TODD LINFORD

As a Relief Society president, I tried to acknowledge every sister on her birthday. I noticed that one of our dear sisters was having a birthday in about a week. The problem was that this sister had just left with her husband on a second mission to the Frankfurt Germany Temple. How was I to get something to her in time for her birthday? I thought about what to send, and decided a card would do. I had plenty of birthday cards and got one out of the cupboard. As I was about to write in the card, I thought how much nicer it would be to put a white handkerchief inside. *Next time I'm at the mall I'll pick one up,* I thought. *The handkerchief will be late by the time it gets to Germany anyway.* Within a few minutes I surprised myself by getting in the car and going to the mall. After I purchased the hankie, I thought, *I'll put it in the mail next time I have to go to the post office.* Later that day I found myself at the post office mailing the card and the handkerchief to Germany.

I thought nothing about it until about a month later when I received this note: "How did you know? After arriving here in Germany, we were told that there was a ride available for us to go to the rededication of the Swiss Temple. I was thrilled for the opportunity, but then remembered that I needed a white handkerchief for the Hosanna Shout. Being so new here, and having no car, I didn't know how to get a handkerchief. I thought I'd just have to use a tissue. We got off work at the temple here in Frankfurt at five and were leaving for Switzerland at seven. As we walked the mile home to our apartment, the problem of the handkerchief was on my mind. We stopped to get the mail, and there was the package from you. You can't imagine the thrill I felt when I opened the card and saw the handkerchief. I felt loved and remembered. Thank you, thank you, thank you. It went right in my bag for the temple dedication."

Elder Ezra Taft Benson said: "Here is happiness. Here is opportunity for personal growth. We can't help others without helping ourselves. The sweetest joys of all come from serving our Heavenly Father in His work. To be a partner in His employ [is] to feel the warmth and peace of His Spirit." (*The Teachings of Ezra Taft Benson,* pp. 449–50.) That sums it up for me—happiness is being sent on an errand by the Spirit.

All Prayers Are Answered

SHERRIE JOHNSON

One mother told of a time when her son was about ten years old. He had wanted and needed a close friend for some time, so when a group of neighborhood boys invited him to go trick or treating he was especially excited. On Halloween day, however, he came home from school utterly dejected. The friends had told him that the group was too large and that he couldn't go with them.

The mother's heart ached as she saw the pain reflected in her son's eyes. It wasn't the first time the group had mistreated him. She knew how anxiously he had looked forward to the event, and now he was shattered. He was too young to go alone and too old to go with mother, but more importantly, he needed a friend. The mother, as she was accustomed to doing, quietly slipped away to her bedroom, shut the door, and knelt down. She then proceeded to pour out her heart to her Father in Heaven. She told him that she knew how hurt and offended her son was and that he needed a special friend. "Show me what to do to help him," she prayed. Her prayer was interrupted by the ringing of the doorbell. She closed her prayer to answer the door and was greeted by a young neighborhood boy who wanted her son to go trick or treating with him. Not all prayers are answered so fast, but all prayers are answered. That is why prayer is one of the most valuable tools we can learn to use as mothers.

End of Rope

KATHLEEN "CASEY" NULL

Raising children is certainly challenging. Who would refute that?

I haven't borne a child yet who didn't at one time or another, usually several times, tax me to the limits of my good nature.

I've had children who wake up screaming at 4:00 A.M., and just as suddenly return to full sleep . . . just about the time I manage to get to them, shivering in the cold.

I've had children who've insisted, no demanded, something so desperately that it took all my energy to try to understand what they were trying to tell me . . . and then to come to understand that they didn't really know themselves.

I've had children with broken hearts and almost broken bones.

I've had children who've dashed to the podium during sacrament after crawling under fourteen families.

I've had children who've failed noisily, and children who've learned painful lessons, and children who've triumphed very quietly.

I've had children who've totally and completely baffled me.

But during one baffling moment it occurred to me that if I can't understand my children, there's only one place to go. To my knees. Our Father knows every one of my children. He knows them well.

At the end of every rope . . . there's prayer.

*N*ourish Both Physically and Spiritually

BARBARA B. SMITH

A woman who must work to care for the needs of her children should learn the essential purposes of life and come to know the Lord and feel his love and direction. Then she can help her children know him and grow to feel secure in our Heavenly Father's love.

One woman who came to this realization wrote to me in these terms:

> Right after my divorce, I determined that I was going to give my children the best of everything . . . I would provide well for them . . . I would substitute in every way for their father. I would take them on picnics, build them a tree house, and play baseball with them. I would not allow them to suffer because of our divorce.
>
> I baked, sewed, ran, played, wrestled. I cleaned, I ironed. I was busy being both mother and father for them.
>
> One evening I put the three of them in the bathtub together while I finished a chore. Then I came back, soaped the youngest, rinsed him off, lifted him from the tub and stood him on a bath mat while I wrapped a bath towel around him. Then I carried him off to the bedroom to put his pajamas on and tuck him into bed. I repeated the process with his brother and sister.
>
> As I bent down to kiss them goodnight, my older son said, "Sing us a song, please."

"Which one?" I asked.

"'Rudolph!'" said the youngest immediately.

"No, 'Johnny Appleseed,'" said his brother.

Then their sister said, "Sing, 'Stay Awake.'"

"I can see if I stay to sing one song, I'll be singing for an hour, and I don't have an hour to spare. So goodnight." I turned off the lights.

"Please sing just one song, Mommy. You can choose the song."

"What about our prayers?"

Firmly, I replied, "I said goodnight and I mean goodnight."

As I walked back to the bathroom to tidy up, I thought of how grateful they would be someday when they were old enough to understand how much I had done for them!

As I entered the room, I stopped short. There on the bath mat were three perfect sets of damp footprints. For one brief moment I thought I saw standing in the footprints the spirits of those precious children I had just tucked into bed. In that instant I saw the foolishness of my ways. I had been so busy providing for the physical needs of their mortal bodies I was neglecting their spirits. I knew then that I had a sacred obligation to nourish both. If I were to clothe them in the latest fashions and give them all that money could buy and fail to tend to their spiritual needs, I could not justifiably account for my awesome responsibility as their mother.

Humbled, I went back to their bedroom. We knelt together in prayer. We all four climbed upon the boys' big bed and sang song after song until I was the only one awake to sing.

One of My Worst Weaknesses

ANITA CANFIELD

One of my worst weaknesses was gossiping, backbiting, judging, and criticizing others. It was a sin that consumed me. It was a weight, a chain of hell that kept me bound down in my own lack of self-esteem. Those who knew me then would never believe that such a person would one day be speaking out on the goodness of others.

It started in high school with all the catty, petty backbiting that young girls do when they are jealous or feel threatened. In college I was even more harsh and critical. During my years as a young married there were those in my life who encouraged, and even enjoyed, this ugly behavior, and I was very much swept away with them.

But because the Holy Ghost can work "a mighty change in . . . our hearts" I was able to see the terrible wrong of this behavior. As I gained more self-esteem, this behavior was unnecessary.

The work of "unlayering" our weaknesses, "peeling" back the worldliness to eventually expose the godliness in each of us, is a process. The Holy Ghost causes our hearts to recognize and desire to change our weaknesses; then, if we but ask for inspiration, he whispers how we might do it.

One day he whispers, "Don't *say* anything bad about anyone anymore." And so for a few years you work and struggle at the "peeling." Another day comes and he whispers, "It's not enough. Another layer must come off. Don't *listen* to anything bad said of others." So for a few more years you struggle to "peel" yet another layer away. And then he whispers again, "It's not enough. You must not *think* of others with judgments." And so a few more years and the peeling continues. Another afternoon and another whisper, "It is not enough. You must *look* for the good in others." So the struggle continues and again you hear another whisper, "Not enough. You must *express* those good thoughts to others." And the unlayering, the struggle to "peel" away goes on.

If you want to turn your weaknesses into strengths, you must first acknowledge your weaknesses with hope. Remember what the Lord said? If men *humble* themselves, if men come unto him, he will show them their weaknesses. He does this with a spirit of love by the power of the Holy Ghost. We end up feeling *inspired,* not discouraged, motivated to be a better person.

$\mathscr{A}$ Preference for Primary

CAMILLE FRONK

Perhaps one reason the Savior admonishes us to "become as little children" (Matthew 18:3) is that children are so pliable, free from pride, and receptive to direction from others. A friend of mine recently reported to a Church leader that she overwhelmingly prefers her calling in the Primary to her previous assignment of teaching adults in Sunday School. "I can understand that," the Church leader responded, "in Primary you still get to work in wet cement."

$\mathcal{S}$trong-Willed Children

NAME WITHHELD

Two strong-willed children taught me how very important it is to listen to the guidance of the Spirit when raising children. Although these children appeared to have similar personalities, evidently they had very different needs that only the Lord understood. Often I felt that different, almost opposite disciplinary methods were needed for them. With the older one the Spirit would whisper, "Don't let him overpower you. He needs to learn to control his strong nature." He thanks me now for the courage he knows I displayed in disciplining him as a youngster.

Using the same methods with his younger brother, however, brought disaster. Trying harder made things even worse. Finally, I asked for heavenly guidance. (I'm sorry to say that it took reaching the end of my wits and endurance before I humbled myself sufficiently to do it.) The answer I received was quite definite: "Just love him. Let him see that you love and value him." Every time I would try to come down on him for misbehavior, the Spirit seemed to pull me back and I was prompted to show him an increase of love (instead of an increase of correction, which I felt more inclined to do). For a long time, our relationship had been less then wonderful, but when I started "just loving" him we began to become closer. He was drawn more and more to the Lord's way despite himself.

Gratitude
and
Appreciation

Discrepancy

SUSAN EVANS McCLOUD

Ruin?
    Amid this quiet springtime eve?
Loss?
    When the sun turns gold this lovely room?
Failure?
    Where children's voices lilt and rise?
Despair?
    Where this gentle beauty fills my eyes?

I Am Grateful for the Trials I Have Not Had

ELAINE CANNON

Ross leaned back in his desk chair and clasped his hands together across his lap. This was not in an act of disinterest, but rather of thoughtfulness. We were talking about Life and if we would be willing to give it another go. What were some specific blessings that had enhanced the experience for him? I prodded. Surely there was much that he could share with others.

Actually, Ross had been dispensing wisdom for half a century. He'd earned every becoming white strand of lush, wiry hair (worn fuller now) in helping others. He had been an attorney and a servant of the Lord. Still incredibly handsome, his face was etched with pleasant lines of expression, like now—unruly thick eyebrows slightly raised; startling blue, snapping eyes slightly squinted; lips pursed together, pressing the tongue against his teeth. It was a signal for me to sit very still and silent while that fertile mind considered the matter before him. I knew this from years of committee and board meetings with him.

Ross had served well and been exceedingly successful. His family had suffered a wide variety of problems and pain, like the year when three people he loved most died untimely deaths. A fluke? Perhaps, but a heartbreak to be dealt with so life could go forward and responsibility not lag. There were the years working in foreign lands away from the lifestyle and the mountain river fishing he enjoyed so much. Besides his own problems, he had seen and heard everything that people in anguish experience. I expected some firm advice to pass along to readers about how to behave in times of trial. As it turned out, his unique reflection seems even more important to include in a book about counting one's blessings rather than swallowing Prozac.

Ross spoke softly, almost reverently, and with evident emotion. "I am thankful for God and his reassuring, guiding hand, and for his gospel. Yes! But I am deeply grateful for the trials . . . I . . . have . . . *not* . . . been . . . given." He paused. "Yes, indeed, I know myself now, and I am glad for what God has spared me."

We talked about being born in other less glorious dispensations of time. He listed certain possible tragic family events, dishonor, public disgraces, limited opportunities for training and service, diminishing faculties with prolonged life, even! Ross had rubbed shoulders with kings and presidents and top executives in both business and academics and with noble women of service. His friends were legion. He knew they did not have what he had in his life. He stressed again that he was most grateful for the blessing he had of not having to live without the support and abundance that the fullness of the gospel clearly gave. He questioned whether he himself would have had the strength to convert to the Church lifestyle midstream. He had noticed the reluctance among his associates to make that step, even though they might have recognized that what Ross had was different. Better.

No doubt about it, Ross's backdoor approach to the blessing-counting exercise teaches an important and comforting point. God, because he knows us, blesses us by not allowing us trials that we could not bear.

My Life Is Not How I Would Have Written It

BARBARA TIMOTHY BOWEN

My life is not how I would have written it. I dreamed about a life more like the one in the movie with a husband who was continually strong, supportive, and healthy and an abundance of adorable children. By the time I was nine, I had names for all 12 of the children I wanted—10 boys and 2 girls (aware of my inability to fix hair, I limited the number of girls). I spent many happy days imagining all the activities and exchanges in our home. I saw myself and my husband in a great team effort to raise this large family of accomplished children and together make a significant contribution to the community.

After a mission and a master's degree I married, at age 26, someone four years younger than myself who had only one year of his undergraduate degree. By this time I had reduced the number of desired children to 7 (I kept the ones with the best names), but I felt confident that my story was beginning to unfold just as I had dreamed. I couldn't have known what chapters God had in mind. Had I read them in advance, I would have shut the book and said that he must have mixed me up with someone else. Either that or he needed a better editor.

I couldn't have known how hard it would be to get the three sons I have to this earth—the infertility, the miscarriages, the interminable medical procedures, and the endless unconsoled tears. I would never have planned on a husband who suffered from depression, struggled in school, and had to war with and eventually die from a malignant brain tumor. I wouldn't have written in a child with a rare eye disease that impaired his vision, or another child who was bright but every year struggled so in school. I wouldn't have included any of the loneliness or heartache. I would have written a much different story.

But without those problems I wouldn't have cheered and praised the heavens when my husband finally graduated from veterinary school and built a national award-winning animal hospital. I wouldn't have rejoiced when our son who had weathered three eye surgeries became our best tennis player, and our son who had struggled to remember the months of the year memorized and performed, flawlessly, eight pages of a script. I wouldn't have known the tenderness in caring for someone who is dying nor wept to see the pure and childlike spirit emerging in a man who was full of love for all of us. I wouldn't have known the depths. I wouldn't have known the heights. And I wouldn't have known that I was part of a perfect story.

$\mathscr{E}$xpressions of Appreciation

MICHAELENE GRASSLI

Each of us needs to feel appreciated. We can never show too much appreciation to others; most of us don't show nearly enough. After a talk I gave on this subject, an energetic and confident young woman spoke to me. She told me how she had spent the past two years as a Primary teacher. She was now in another calling, but I could tell from her demeanor that she probably had been a wonderful teacher. She said she had enjoyed the children and she had enjoyed what she had learned from the lessons, but—and this was fascinating to me, coming from such an outgoing, confident woman—she said, "Those two years were the loneliest two years of my life."

What happens inside someone who feels like that? They have to be very self-motivated and firm in the faith to continue on in the calling and in the Church. Leaders cannot do everything for the people with whom they are serving, but they can do some things, and one is giving adequate support and sincere appreciation.

Even President Spencer W. Kimball longed for expressions of appreciation. "I find myself hungering and thirsting for just a word of appreciation or of honest evaluation from my superiors and my peers. I want no praise; I want no flattery; I am seeking only to know if what I gave was acceptable." (*The Teachings of Spencer W. Kimball,* ed. Edward L. Kimball [Salt Lake City: Bookcraft, 1982], p. 489.)

Contrasts

HELEN M. TERRY

I used to think the fabric
Of my days should be
A web of bright and shining strands,
Unshaded, shadow-free.
But years have yielded wisdom;
I have learned, instead,
We weave the tapestry of life
With variegated thread.

Gratitude

ALBERT L. ZOBELL, JR.

There is a story of an ungrateful elderly woman who grumbled at everything and everybody. Her bishop had determined to try to find something about which this woman had no complaint. He thought he had found it in her crop of potatoes, which that year was the finest for miles around.

"For once you must be pleased," the bishop said with a smile as he met the woman in front of her cottage. "Everybody's saying how splendid your potatoes are this year."

The woman glowered at him as she answered: "They're not so bad. But where's the bad potatoes for the pigs?"

The Hammer

MARILYNNE TODD LINFORD

Ellen told about the day her fix-it husband needed her to help repair the roof. Of course she had her own Saturday work to do inside, but there she was lying flat on her tummy on the roof, handing tools to her husband, who was on a ladder a few feet below, repairing something under the eaves. According to Ellen's account, her husband seemed to forget that she was a volunteer doing something she didn't want to do. He became frustrated if she handed him a wrong tool or gave him a tool wrong end first. He asked for the hammer. She handed it to him with a little extra thrust. She heard it crash to the ground. Oops! She waited to hear him get after her. She waited and waited. Finally she knew she should apologize, so she scooted to the edge to say she was sorry. Looking over the edge of the roof, she saw the hammer on the ground lying next to her husband. Yep, she had knocked him out.

To a Mother-in-Law in Israel

ALICE BRADY MYERS

There is a thought
Finely wrought
In gratitude's chamber within my heart,

That had you borne Naomi's grief
And I been Moab's daughter,
Your kindness would have drawn me thence
Where I could call you Mother.

But Israel's home
Is both our own,
Our seed of faith by One Hand sown.

So, as Rebekah, I came unto
Your tent of charity,
Where, with Sarah's tender grace,
You offered love to me.

Finding Peace and Balance in Life

You're the Princess

BARBARA TIMOTHY BOWEN

One evening while I was standing at the sink, which was so piled with dishes I wasn't sure there was a sink, except for the sound of running water underneath—stringy hair in my face; an old, food-stained apron hanging over my shoulders; feeling overburdened, overwhelmed, overweight, and unloved—my three-year-old, who had been sent to bed five times already, peeked into the kitchen, wearing his Superman cape and Burger King crown. Before I could scold him one more time to get back to bed, he exclaimed, "Mommy, Mommy, I da pwince, and you da . . . you da . . ."

"I the what?" I responded, still a little exasperated, but softening at this child's tender petition.

"I da pwince," he continued, "and you da, oh, what's da girl?"

"The girl?" I asked. "You mean the princess?"

"Yeah!" he shouted joyously, then looked up at me with bright, twinkling eyes and said, "I da pwince an' you da pwincess, and let's dance!"

As I picked up my little boy and we waltzed through the kitchen that evening, I didn't look back at the plates in the sink or the plates in my life. In that moment, I was the princess, and I was dancing with the prince. In that moment, I saw only love.

Thanks, Jacob, I Needed That

JANENE WOLSEY BAADSGAARD

My family does our best to keep this old planet from spinning off its axis. Each week we have a planning session which consists mainly of Mom standing next to a giant paper calendar taped to the refrigerator while each family member yells out what they have on their agenda for the week.

Now, don't get me wrong, we are not one of those boring Franklin families who try to give their children a day planner on their first birthday. This is our way of staying in touch with each other, our feeble attempt to make some sense and order out of our hectic lives.

I'm telling you this because a while back something happened to change my idea about sense and order. While I was busy writing up my husband's meetings on the calendar, my five-year-old son quietly tiptoed to my side and whispered, "Mom, on Tuesday write, 'Jacob has to do . . . nothing.'" I wasn't paying attention and he repeated a little louder, "Mom, on Tuesday write, 'Jacob has to do . . . nothing.'"

When Jacob gets something on his mind, I've found it's much easier to do what he says than pay the consequences. So instead of reasoning with him about the silliness of taking up limited calendar space, I quickly wrote exactly what he said in minute script on the corner of the square marked Tuesday. Jacob liked the look and power of his new plans and continued in his boss-to-secretary voice, "On Wednesday write, 'Jacob has to . . . play with friends, goof off, and have fun.'"

I began dutifully taking his dictation for Wednesday, then stopped. "Now Jacob, we're trying to do our family planning for this week. Don't interrupt me any more," I said before Jacob could quite complete his further instructions for Thursday.

Well, we finished our planning session, the clean white numbered squares quickly filling up with commitments for every day of the week. Later we dashed into our bedtime bustle routine.

It wasn't until after breakfast the next morning that I glanced over at the calendar on the refrigerator and began reading the mass of activities that would fill my family's week. I felt like crawling back into bed and pulling the blankets over my head. Juggling the demands and commitments of nine people is no small matter. Then I noticed that tiny notation in the upper corner of the square marked Tuesday: "Jacob has to do . . . nothing." Jacob's plans suddenly looked pretty good.

I wondered if maybe we'd all be better off if we carefully pulled out our leather-bound day planners and efficiently wrote in the square reserved for Tuesday, "Janene (you can fill in your own name here) *has* to do . . . nothing." And I think we'd all feel a little less tired if we regularly wrote in the square marked Wednesday, "Have to play with friends, goof off, and have fun."

I know, I know—somebody has to make a living and fix supper. But the problem is we start filling up our lives with so many shoulds and oughts, we sometimes forget we don't really *have* to do anything. What we do is by choice. I'm not sure I'm ready to accept that fact, but truth it remains. We don't have to do anything. We choose to live as we live, and if we don't like it, we can stop and shout, "Hey! Hold it! I want to rethink this for a minute."

After all the thinking is over and all the shoulds and oughts are pushed aside for a time, I think a lot of us would actually just pick up where we left off and keep doing what we were doing all along. Only this time we'd do it with a new twist. We'd now live as we live not because we *have* to but because we *choose* to.

Thanks, Jacob. I needed that.

For Example

KATHRYN KAY

What else is there to do
except stop crying,
regird myself, with faith restrengthening—
what's life itself except continued trying?
For instance, look at winter . . . look at spring!

ℒovely, Lonely Home

KATHLEEN "CASEY" NULL

Sigh? Sigh?" My daughter stood at the door wistfully repeating her request.

"Sigh" is her one-year-old word for "outside." But it also meant, I knew, that she wanted me to put her in the swing and push her.

An hour earlier, my husband had taken all three boys to their grandparents, and I saw it as my chance to clean up. And I'd been cleaning like a tumultuous whirlwind, delighting that there was only one little person underfoot.

I was tossing out rusty bottle caps, knocking spit wads off the bedroom walls, stripping beds, mopping muddy stains off floors. Who would've ever thought I'd find housework such a delightful activity?

I was just about to tackle bicycle grease on the carpet when I heard my daughter's wistful little "sighs."

"He should've taken her too," I began to grumble. "How can I keep this house clean enough to keep the health department away with the kids constantly working so hard to mess it up—and then interrupting me when I try to get at it again."

"Sigh? Sigh?" My daughter looked at me shyly.

"If I take her outside and push her for a while, I won't have time to get out this bicycle grease." I knew that even if I worked non-stop until midnight I wouldn't finish it all—but I *did* want to get as much of it done as I could.

"Sigh . . ." She looked longingly out of the window.

I knew I'd give in. The dust will wait, but my children won't.

I pushed her on the swing. My insides giggled as she giggled out loud and her feathery wisps of hair wafted on the wind.

"Yes," I thought, "if it weren't for my kids, I'd have a lovely home.

"Instead of baseball mitts, jars of insects, and building blocks about, there'd be some pre-Columbian artifacts, Cézanne paintings, and lush greenery in every corner.

"I could do housework once a week, and it would stay done until it was time to do it again. The walls would be handprint and footprint free. I could eat at a table with china and no spilled milk."

Yes, I'd live in a very lovely . . . very lonely home.

$\mathscr{B}$ob and Weave

ELAINE L. JACK

A friend of mine recently came to visit, looking like the loser of a twelve-round prize fight.

"What is wrong?" I asked, as she burst into tears. The trouble was that one of her neighbors had lambasted her repeatedly over a matter concerning their daughters, who were best friends. It seems my friend's daughter had offended the neighbor's daughter, and the neighbor had marched right over and let my friend have it. What offended her was first being treated as if she were responsible for her daughter's comments and finally being talked to as if she were a child herself.

My friend said, "Elaine, it's bad enough to have such an unpleasant encounter once, but she won't let it go. She's talked to me four times about the same trouble, even though the girls have forgotten the whole episode. What should I do?"

My answer: "Bob and weave."

"What do you mean?" my confused friend asked.

I suggested, "Don't take offense at this. Isn't this the same neighbor who was so angry when your son cracked her kitchen window with a baseball? He paid for the damage, but she insisted on telling you several times how distressed she was. After she'd vented her feelings, she was fine.

"She apparently needs to vent when she's angry, and it seems she doesn't get it all out the first time. Just because she needs to say it more than once doesn't mean you have to stand there like a punching bag waiting for her to hit you again. Don't stand there flat-footed—keep moving. Bob and weave like champion prize fighters. They don't just stand in one place when someone approaches with boxing gloves on. They take some initiative, and so should you. Write her a nice note explaining your feelings. Invite them over for a family picnic. Go shopping together. Tell her the next good joke you hear. Bake her some brownies and take them to her while they're still warm. Pour her a nice glass of milk, and when she takes that first mouthful, hurry and explain how much you'd like to be her friend. Then treat her as if she were your best friend. No matter what she does, keep moving. Do what you can, maintain a sense of humor, then let it go."

Having received this counsel from another friend when I was a young mother, I know it's sound. I share it with all of you. Take initiative, do good, enjoy humor. And, please, avoid offense.

$\mathscr{M}$y Particular Love Is Music

LINDA J. EYRE

$\mathbf{M}$y particular love is music. I was a string major in college, and though I was terrified to play by myself, I loved playing
in groups. Many years ago, when we were first married, I found
a wonderful group of "kindred spirits" while we lived in Washington, D.C., with whom I played in a string quartet. It was their
love and support that changed my terror of performing into a
love for it. The group consisted of another violinist, Cheryln; a
cellist, Carolyn; and a violist, another Carolyn. (I always regretted
that my name wasn't Marilyn.)

Richard and I moved away from these "soul sisters" for almost
eight years, and then went back to Washington to find that they
were all still there, ready to play. Our circumstances had changed
somewhat by then, however: Among the four of us we had
twenty-six children and two grandchildren.

After our first rehearsal we were so thrilled to be playing
together again that we pledged ourselves to prepare a forty-five-
minute program to be presented in three months (before we
moved again) at the Washington Temple Visitors' Center.

No one would believe the riotous times we had together at
rehearsals. If we could have taped the practices, unedited they
would easily have been funnier than any sitcom you see on TV.

In the first place, we rehearsed with at least seven preschoolers under foot. (We learned to practice with our feet on our
stands to keep the crawling babies from tipping them over.) One
Carolyn was the president of a large women's organization and
dashed in between meetings to play. The other Carolyn had to
drive forty-five minutes one way to get to the rehearsals and

came in her teenager's car (which looked a lot like it had just been through the trash masher) in between car-pools and the frantic schedules of her eight children. Cheryln had a nursing baby, and though we tried to convince her to learn to nurse and play the violin at the same time (mothers have to learn to do almost any *other* two actions simultaneously) she opted to hum her part while we played and she nursed.

Someone was always late, and there were usually two or three rounds of calls before we worked out a satisfactory "next rehearsal" time. But when we got together—did we ever have a great time! We loved making beautiful music together.

Every rehearsal was an adventure. About every eight minutes one of the roving pack of little ones needed a Band-Aid, a rescue from a bad dog, a peanut-butter sandwich, a clean diaper, or a mediator for negotiations on toys. Other than that, they danced together to the music and once even took off all their clothes and had a great romp in the little plastic swimming pool in the back yard. At the end of the movement, Carolyn often found my baby hanging on the endpin of her cello, gazing up at her.

We performed many times together during those few months and it was always an unbelievable hassle, but the night of our *big* recital topped them all in more ways than one.

One Carolyn had just returned from a two-week trip to Hawaii, China, and Egypt, and we had practiced ferociously the last two days. The night of the performance she called to ask if I could drive, as she had just realized that the insurance had expired on her car. I had been about to call her to tell her that there was a flat tire on our car and we had no spare. I had been frantically packing all day in 90-degree heat and 85-percent humidity, as the moving men were coming the next day. We decided on the uninsured car.

When we got there, a little later than planned, the other Carolyn and Cheryln, who came from the other direction, still had not arrived, and when they did (huffing and puffing and redfaced) one explained that her husband had been held up and didn't get home to take over the kids and the other had a van full of cases of grapefruit that her kids were selling for a fund-raising project. Somehow the brake had released and the van had coasted across the street and into the neighbor's tree, scattering grapefruits everywhere, not to mention the damage to car and tree. We all got the giggles about being so "true to the end" and then settled down to the seriousness of the task ahead.

I must admit that my eyes filled with tears during the last piece we played, "Canon in D" by Johann Pachelbel, a work that we all loved. My mind wandered back to all the wonderful times we'd had together talking and playing and enjoying in spite of the adversity. How easy it would have been for any one to say, "I'm too busy. Let's do that when the kids are grown."

Kindness

MARILYNNE TODD LINFORD

I once heard the story of a woman who decided to be perfect for just one day. As things inevitably started to go wrong, she found perfection wasn't possible, because the world is full of imperfect people. She became discouraged. A few months later she decided to try being not perfect but kind for a day. As the inevitable again began to test her goal, she found much to her delight that in spite of the things she couldn't control, she still could be kind. At the end of the day she wrote in her journal, "I succeeded in being kind all day and, surprising as it sounds, I was nearly perfect." Affirmative action creates an in-charge feeling. It's a two-sided blessing. Both giver and receiver are enriched.

Thanksgiving Treasure

JANENE WOLSEY BAADSGAARD

Most of my Thanksgiving Day memories are steaming with oven-roasted turkey or fresh yeast rolls. There are always crowds of people wandering through those memories too . . . uncles with whiskers and bad breath who want to kiss you . . . brothers and sisters who cap their teeth with black olives and blow bubbles in their fruit punch. The grown-ups are always murmuring in the dining room, stopping only long enough to say, "All right, you kids, settle down out there!"

But one year there were no turkeys, no relatives, no black olives, and no fruit punch. My husband and I had plans to go to Grandma's for the usual feast, but a busy nightlong vigil made for a quick change of plans.

On the night before Thanksgiving Day, each of our children had taken a turn becoming ill with the stomach flu. My husband and I ran from bed to bed. We had the washing machine going all night.

Just when it appeared we had seen the worst of it and the children were starting to go back to sleep, it hit my husband and me. By morning the whole family looked like death warmed over.

That Thanksgiving the children were too weak to play or wiggle or even fight. There were no visitors. Nobody wanted to catch what we had. There was no feast. No one could keep anything down even if anyone could get up and fix it.

It was a quiet day. There was no TV blaring in the corner of the room or radio broadcasting from the bookshelf. The rocking chair creaked slowly next to the piano in the living room while my husband took turns rocking the children to sleep.

As I sat on our worn sofa stroking a child's small head in my lap and cradling another in the bend of my arm, I did a lot of thinking—thinking about what I was grateful for. I wasn't distracted by football games, turkey, or relatives.

As I rubbed my child's sweaty forehead and looked into his eyes, it occurred to me that it wasn't the neighborhood I lived in, or the new carpet or lack of it, that really mattered. Everything that really mattered was who I loved and who loved me.

The whole richness of life was contained in the embryotic relationships that were growing, developing, and changing within the walls of my own home. My relationships with people, not my possessions or positions, would ultimately tell the meaning of my life.

I realized that most of the problems our family faced came from being overcommitted, from having too much to do. Our relationships suffered when we couldn't bring ourselves to say no to other people, to properly *unorder* our lives so there was enough time to take walks together, play board games on the kitchen table, tell jokes while we scrubbed the pots and pans, or snuggle in the rocking chair as we watched the stars appear in the night sky.

It really isn't quality time but lots of unscheduled quantity time that matters. We spend the most time with what we truly love.

We didn't dress or eat or even talk much that day. My thoughts were slow, unhurried, and singular. I looked at my husband and my children differently that day, as if I were seeing them for the first time. I noticed the unusual upward turn of my husband's brow, the circular mixture of blue, green, and brown in my daughter's eyes, the soft, satin feel of my baby's cheeks.

My family was all that seemed real that day. The rest of the world seemed out of focus, somewhere out there in the distance. Everything that really mattered was rocking quietly next to the piano or snuggled deep in my arms. I was intensely aware of the swelling emotion I felt for each child and for my husband. I loved them more than I could express.

That evening, we all sat around the kitchen table and took turns telling each other what we were grateful for. Later, we bowed our heads as our three-year-old led us in prayer.

"Heavenly Father, thank thee for all the guys and Mom and Dad. Amen."

Our feast that evening consisted of one banana Popsicle per person. I've never had a day or a banana Popsicle that tasted so good.

$\mathcal{S}$unday Incident

ANITA CANFIELD

I asked my friend if she would share her experience of how she discovered humility through gratitude. She wrote the following. (The names have been changed.)

Sunday Incident

One Sunday afternoon my husband and I were spending some time with our family, trying to keep six active children busy in Sabbath activities.

Dave and I were sitting on the couch in the living room listening to Jill play hymns on the piano. One of our teenagers, Kevin, walked through the room and draped himself over the other couch. Another teenage son, Brad, came in to ask our opinion of a social event he wanted to attend. Our two younger boys, Sean and Matt, were playing a game at the kitchen table. The littlest one, Jana, was dressing her dolls beside me on the couch.

The kitchen timer sounded from the oven, signaling that the roast for dinner was done.

Dave and I rose and headed for the kitchen to put dinner on the table. We passed Jill at the piano, inviting her to come help with dinner and thanking her for her playing. Jana followed us with her dolls.

We passed Kevin draped over the couch, joked with him, and arrived at the kitchen.

Dave began to carve the roast, Jill to cut up cantaloupe, and I to supervise the younger boys in setting the table.

As we began to work in the small, U-shaped kitchen, we

stumbled over each other at every turn. We had to continually reach across each other to get things out of the cabinets. At every turn we bumped elbows, and had to say "excuse me." I felt my tension rising.

As I directed the younger boys in setting the table and bringing to them items to put on the table, they fooled around a little, and my tension rose some more.

During this bustling around, Kevin undraped himself from the couch and wandered into the kitchen. He watched the bustling around.

"Mom," he said, "You'd better do something about Sean and Matt when you go on your trip with Dad next week. They really gave the babysitter a hard time last time you went."

Little Jana piped up, "Mom, I don't want you to go on a trip. I am sad when you go."

Her big eyes looked yearningly at me, and my tension went up another notch.

Meanwhile I settled differences between Sean and Matt as they set the table. I angrily kicked out of my path a tennis shoe and sock which had been left there.

"Dave, we've *got* to get that list of family rules made—these children are so untrained!"

He answered, "I'm always available for discussion."

My tension rose again. "You *say* you're always available, but you're not!"

I slammed down the basket of rolls on the table and just then I noticed that Kevin had opened his mouth to join in the fray, and Jana was about to cry.

Suddenly I felt overwhelming anger and couldn't bear to deal with one more thing. The wave of anger was so intense that I was shaking, and yet it seemed to have come out of nowhere. I stopped Kevin's words before they were out of his mouth and I grabbed my purse and notebook from the kitchen desk and blurted out, "I just can't stand this any longer! I'm leaving to go make up a set of family rules and I'm not coming back until I get it done!"

I headed for the front door, propelled by a force I felt I couldn't control.

On the way I was vaguely aware of the children's bewildered faces, and my husband's look of concerned surprise.

I didn't look back but went straight for the car. I drove to a secluded place where I like to go and think.

There I bowed my head, still shaking, and pleaded with the Lord to help me understand what was wrong. "Please Heavenly Father, I don't know why I'm so angry. Please help me."

The thought came into my mind, *Write down your thoughts.*

I immediately opened my notebook, took a fresh page, and started to write down every thought I could remember having during the course of that afternoon. Soon the page was filled as I went back over the moments and replayed them in my mind.

Then I stopped and took a good look at what I had written on the page. It horrified me. There was a long list of fearful, defeated, judgmental, worried thoughts.

I'm worried about Kevin's being lazy.
I'm worried about Brad; I'm not close enough to him.
Our house is too small.
I'll never be able to train children adequately in this tiny kitchen.
Family improvement is too slow; we'll never make it.
I won't survive long enough until things (maybe?) change.
I'm worried about going on the trip with Dave.
What clothes will I take?
Will I do a good enough job as hostess to the other people?
Sean and Matt will misbehave when I'm gone.
Jana will be sad without me.
This whole trip is a problem.
The family is so untrained.
Everywhere I turn is pressure.

And the list went on, describing my emotional response to

everything said or done that afternoon. No *wonder* I felt angry, upset, and discouraged that things would never change.

With the realization of the cause of the anger came a sudden calm. And then the next question formed: "Heavenly Father, I see what happened. But what can I *do* about it? How can I get rid of these feelings?

The thought came to me, *Write some secure thoughts.*

I wondered. What are secure thoughts? Well, I guess any thought that gives me hope in the situation.

So I took a new page and began to write every thought that gave me hope and comfort that I could overcome the situation. One by one the thoughts came—sweet, secure thoughts.

> We can always repent (or change).
> We can always grow and improve.
> Heavenly Father will give us light and knowledge about how to solve our problems.
> He will sustain us *while* we're changing.
> He will give us sufficient strength to meet the demands of *today*—one at a time.
> I have many blessings—count them:
> A husband who loves me,
>   who is willing to change,
>   who is wise;
> Children who are healthy and who love me;
> Friends I could call upon if necessary;
> Good health;
> Many comforts;
> Access to truth through Heavenly Father;
> Opportunities to grow.

And the list went on—sweet thoughts of faith, as if someone were beckoning me on, saying, "Come on, you can do it."

The sweetest feeling of peace came over me. Suddenly the anger and anxiety had disappeared, and in it's place was love—

Love for myself, my family, and the Lord.

"Yes, I *can* do it."

I bowed my head again, to thank him, and drove home to face the challenge.

Things That Ease the Strain

EMMA LOU THAYNE

Have a perm that's wash-and-wear, not even blow-dried. Nice. Especially since I'm a motor moron with anything but a brush. I remember too well the back-combed pouf of my young motherhood that I didn't dare even scratch and hated to sleep on and had to go to Robert Steur's college of magic twice a week for a dollar in order to stay "presentable"!

• Make peace with dieting. Maintain a comfort zone. I'm better at abstinence than moderation. Weekends and other people's food are for indulging, Mondays are for *my* fare and *my* diet. But I have to keep a sense of humor along with a sense of my proportion.

Wonderful old jokes that apply: After forty years of dieting, I should be worn on a charm bracelet. Or, the five stages of a woman's wishing: (1) to grow up, (2) to fill out, (3) to slim down, (4) to hold it in, and (5) to heck with it.

• Exercise can be the saving grace—fun exercise. Without it I wither, go stiff, am subject to injury both physical and psychological. With it I get to frolic, something easy to forget in adulthood, as I let go of whatever else might be assaulting my sense of equilibrium. And somehow it's a lot more fun with someone you can get the giggles with even as you chase a ball or walk a track or bike the neighborhood.

Every minute I save can be my own. It's so much easier to block out time for emergencies than for things I just plain want to do. Was anyone ever too busy to go to a funeral? Why not time with a very alive friend for talking about a book or going to a movie or just calling on the phone?

• Sanity must come before obligation. People respect a "circuits on overload" or "I'm on sabbatical" better than any fabricated excuse. I cannot run faster than I can—and I can do only so much, less now than I used to. Staying up all night, for instance. I used to do it once a week. In those delicious, quiet hours I'd write, read, refinish furniture, maybe even freeze raspberries. It gave me the extra "day" I always longed for, that nobody else knew about. If I kept active the next day and went to bed at a normal time, I got along just fine.

But that's not so anymore. Still tyrannized by too many and too much to love, I can get to where the too much is not "done in wisdom and order," as I try to "run faster than [I have] strength" (Mosiah 4:27). But saying no, especially to myself, is a learned ability, whose gentleness I have come to cherish almost as much as I did those all-nighters of not so long ago.

• Make friends with technology. Learning something new can replace any number of "used to's." I resisted an electric typewriter because I had loved my jumpy old portable. Then a self-correcting typewriter came along—it too took a lot of white-out to come around to. But now! Those are "used to's," and my computer is my buddy. Oh, to fix up my spelling, my typos, my uncanny aptitude for making a mistake in the very last line of a poem! My trusty Mac SE is my genie, my intrigue. The day a word processor took hold of me was another birthday.

At first an intimidating, frustrating complex of commands and errors—all mine—this amazement has become my entree to the last of my century. As have a microwave, a computer to open my car (impossible to lock in my keys!), tapes to go with me anywhere to instruct, inspire, and carry me off on words or music I heard only in lecture or concert halls even ten years ago. So much. So wondrous. If only I am willing to move on.

• Let others do what they can do as well as or better than I can. Especially now that both energy and time are becoming my most precious commodities, I must delegate, hire it out, save myself for what only I can do—and get good enough at it that what I *have* to do is what I *want* to do.

Finding Joy and Humor in Life

Find Joy in the Service of God

MICHAELENE GRASSLI

I was in a Primary General Board committee meeting when a secretary from our office entered the room and motioned to me to step out into the hall. When I did so, she handed me a note that had a Church office extension number on it. Now, as a board member, I was not accustomed to having the secretaries summon me, nor was it usual for me to be requested to call someone in Church headquarters. My husband had occasionally had business in what was then the building department, so I thought maybe he was in the office building calling for me.

The secretary had recognized the extension number. Curious, she stood right by me as I made the call. As the voice on the other end answered, my eyes widened and I mouthed silently, "The *First Presidency's* office!"

Brother D. Arthur Haycock, then secretary to the First Presidency, came on the line and greeted me, "Good afternoon, Sister Grassli. How are you?"

What a question! At that moment I didn't even know my name, much less how I was.

Brother Haycock told me that President Spencer W. Kimball wished to meet with me. He gave me instructions as to how to find the office, since I had not been in the administration building where most General Authority offices are located.

My heart pounded as I made my way to the administration building. I couldn't imagine why I had been summoned. I was the youngest, least experienced, least talented, and least visible or vocal of the board members. What could President Kimball possibly want?

With knees shaking, I thought of the dress I had put on that morning in a rush to leave the house. After I had dressed, I had remembered why I hadn't worn it for a while. It was old and had a small hole near the hem, burned by a cinder that had popped from the fireplace one day as I was standing near it. *Oh well,* I had said to myself. *I'm late. It's just a committee meeting. Nobody will notice it.* Now I was sorry I had not stopped to change. *It's not worthy of an audience with a prophet,* I thought.

As Brother Haycock ushered me into President Kimball's office, I was enveloped by a feeling of calm peace. We were introduced, President Kimball shook my hand warmly, and I sat down in a chair across the desk from the prophet. He didn't even look at the dress I was wearing. Silly me.

"Sister Grassli, today we've called Sister Dwan Young to be the new Primary president and Sister Virginia Cannon to be the new first counselor. We'd like you to serve as the second counselor."

I was speechless. He waited. I could hardly breathe.

"Sister Grassli?" Pause. "Do you feel you can accept the call, Sister Grassli?"

"Yes. Yes, of course, President Kimball." I couldn't imagine how I could do it, but I was not accustomed to declining a call to serve.

Then there was an especially long pause. I didn't know what to do next. President Kimball looked at me. I looked back. He looked some more. I started to get uneasy. My thoughts turned to my inadequacies, faults, and failings—all the reasons why I thought I was not a good choice for the call. As these thoughts played out in my head, I remembered hearing that prophets can see things sometimes that others cannot. I thought, *He's seeing my imperfections!* As President Kimball continued to sit silently, I was sure he was scrutinizing me.

Then suddenly the thought popped into my mind, *Oh! He's sorry already!*

Thinking—erroneously, of course—that a prophet needed an invitation to call someone to repentance, I asked, "President Kimball, do you have any counsel for me?"

"Well, yes, I do."

This is it, I thought.

But he didn't call me to repentance. He said simply, "Find joy in the service of God."

The Bitter and the Sweet

JANENE WOLSEY BAADSGAARD

I brought you some peaches," she said when I answered the front door. "I don't do much canning any more, now that there's only me to do for. I thought your family could use these. They're clingstone, but they taste good."

I took the peaches and ushered her through the door toward the kitchen. After I'd transferred the peaches into my own bowl, I slipped the empty bowl back into her hands and thanked her.

"How've you been doing?" she asked, making herself comfortable in a chair next to the kitchen table. "I've been thinking about you lately and getting a bit lonely to talk to you. I see you at church, but that doesn't seem good enough."

"I'm fine," I answered. "I felt the baby move yesterday. The doctor says everything looks good this time. We have our fingers crossed."

School had recently started, canning season was in full swing, my church responsibilities had taken extra time lately, and I hadn't even noticed it had been weeks since we'd talked together. Now that I could relax and think about it, I'd missed her too. I sat down opposite her at the table and took a breather from folding clothes, washing dishes, and chasing my preschoolers around the house after they had painted each other's bellies with oil paint. It felt good to be near her, my eighty-six-year-old neighbor and good friend, Edna Gerber.

She'd been through these growing years with me. Whenever things got a little crazy and I thought I might blow my top at the children, I'd always suggest they go visit Mrs. Gerber. They always came back with a grin and a piece of candy drooling down their chins.

With a few minutes of quiet to myself, I could handle the rest of the day after they returned. She had rescued me many, many times over the years. I doubted she knew that.

"How've you been?" I asked. "How's your hernia? Does it still get you up at night?"

"It's not too bad," she said. "The doctor said the risks of surgery at my age would be greater than just enduring the pain. It gets me up at night, but I take something warm, turn on the radio, and I can usually get back to sleep. But I feel so guilty because I sleep in until eight o'clock and don't seem to be able to get as much done as I'd like."

Edna's hair is soft and gray, her skin wrinkled and smooth. She wears thick glasses that help with her failing eyesight and a hearing aid to help with advancing deafness.

"But you know, everybody has something bothering them or paining them," Edna continued. "This is just mine. I used to think life would be so easy when I got my family all raised, that all my troubles would be pretty much over. But I've discovered problems don't go away—they just change. I think a person's only happy if they live happily even with troubles and pain, knowing there's no easy time of life. Life's full of good and bad, but it's knowing a few hard times that makes the good times seem so sweet."

That night, my growing family shared the peaches she had brought over. As the sweetness lingered on my tongue, I looked around the table at my children, smiled contentedly, and took a deep breath.

"Pass the milk, you geek," my eight-year-old yelled across the table. "Can't you hear me? You deaf?"

"Mom, tell Joseph to quit kicking me," Arianne insisted.

Someone spilled their milk, and someone flipped their peas across the table with their fork while the three-year-old stood up in his chair, tumbled backward, and banged his head on the floor.

Amid the screams I heard the words again: *Problems don't go away—they just change. But it's knowing the hard times that makes the good times seem so sweet.*

I hurried for a cold washrag from the sink to soothe a bruised head.

Even after the children were herded out of the kitchen and the dish washing was done, the sweet scent of Edna's peaches still filled the room.

I Just Don't Think It's Worth It

EARLENE BLASER

When the staff divided holidays, I quickly volunteered for New Year's Eve, and then begrudgingly had to also accept Christmas Eve. If they only knew how fun those nights were at my house, they would have shut the hospital down. Thanksgiving was my first holiday to work. It wasn't so bad at work, not many accidents, everyone fairly cheerful, and Steve home cooking a full-course dinner for ten. The family waited patiently (ha ha) for me to finish my shift, and we ate at four in the afternoon. After everyone had wolfed down their meal in fifteen minutes and hurriedly left the table, Steve just sat there stunned. He looked at all the dishes, then the kitchen, and said, "I just don't think it's worth it; I cooked for eight hours and nobody cared." I loved it. It turned out to be a great holiday.

A Matter of Attitude

BROOKIE PETERSON

Once, when my husband and I were spending a few days in the mission home in the Dominican Republic, I met a young woman about age twenty-four. She and her husband, a medical student, were from Utah. They had a little boy who was probably nine or ten months old. I asked her, "What has been the hardest thing for you to adjust to since coming to the island?" She told me that at first she had been excited to travel and anxious to have new experiences, but the culture shock was great and gradually she became discouraged. As her feelings of dislike for her new surroundings grew, she became quite unhappy.

Perhaps the hardest time came one day when she was preparing to wash a bucket of diapers. To her dismay she found that the lid had been left slightly ajar and the diapers were covered with maggots. If she had been at home she would have burned them or dug a hole and buried them, but in the Dominican Republic she simply had to clean them. It wasn't possible to get any more.

By the time she went home for Christmas, she could hardly have been more depressed. Her mother soon recognized the daughter's feelings. She told her daughter that she alone could decide whether her experience would be happy or miserable during the next four years. "You can 'bloom where you're planted' or spend the time longing for your husband's graduation so you can return home—it will be your decision," her mother emphasized.

The young wife had a clear understanding of her mother's words and could imagine how miserable it would be to feel unhappy the whole time she was away from home. She decided that wasn't what she wanted and was able to change her whole attitude. Through her discussion with her mother (her mother being someone she trusted) as well as through logic, she gained the strength to know she could not only tolerate but enjoy a place and a people who were so significantly different. She told me that since the time of her return to Dominica she had felt peaceful and interested in her surroundings. Though conditions had not improved, she was now in charge and involved in making her life joyful.

$\mathscr{B}$at Man

KAREN J. ASHTON

When things don't go exactly as you would wish, or when there is a minor tragedy, don't let anger take over. Pause for a moment and find the humor in the situation. Think how you are going to tell this story in ten years' time. Remember that crisis plus time equals humor. When you project forward like this you can actually enjoy the humor up front. You also store it in a humor bank where you can take it out and laugh over and over again.

One morning I found the name "Spencer" written in black crayon over my son Spencer's bed. I marched down to the family room, confronted five-year-old Spencer, and demanded to know why he would do such a thing! He looked up at me for a moment and then asked, "How did you know it was me?"

I could hardly keep from laughing. "Because you wrote your name," I answered with a smile. It took both of us several minutes to scrub his name off the wall. The very next morning I discovered the name "Bat Man" written in the same place. As I stared at the wall I couldn't help but shake my head and smile at the thought process of a five-year-old. I knew this was going to make a great story. In fact, I told it at his wedding breakfast. By the way, Spencer did scrub the wall again.

$\mathcal{A}$ Proper Perspective

GORDON T. ALLRED

Sharon sighed, glancing at me with her turquoise eyes. "Well, here's the bitter truth, if you're man enough to hear it," she began.

"I'm not," I replied, "but go ahead."

She sighed again, consulting our accounts. "All right: first of all there were the two birthdays this month—that comes to seventy-nine dollars." I flinched but maintained some semblance of composure. "And then there was that twenty to get Chester out of the dog pound. He followed the kids down to the supermarket again, and of course the dog nabber was waiting."

"I've warned them," I explained, "warned them a million times to keep him on his line, but it's hopeless."

Sharon continued, "Robby has eleven cavities and Amy has nine."

"You've got to be kidding," I groaned, "you've got to."

"I kid you not," she responded.

I leaned on the table with my elbows, head clasped in my hands. "Rob just broke his two front teeth in half last month. How is it possible for a kid to fall down in the middle of a deserted street and break out both front teeth without another mark on him?"

"Dad?" a voice came.

"Just be glad it wasn't worse," came the reply.

I was in no mood to be glad. I was reveling in self-pity. "Dad?" the voice came. Or was it simply an echo of the imagination?

"Hey, Daa-ud?"

I closed my eyes and began massaging my temples. A sinus headache was in the works, maybe even the flu, and there was a faint ringing inside my skull like the final tones of a doorbell. "Well, thank the good Lord we have our insurance," I said stoically.

"Sweetheart," Shary answered. The word was saturated with compassion and warning; it upset me very badly. "I'm afraid I have to tell you something—well, something rather painful. I mean, well, the insurance—ah, you remember that letter about the grace period? Well, we're no longer saved by grace."

My eyelids clenched tightly shut. "Oh no, surely not! You've got to be kid—" I caught myself, having tried that tack before.

"Maybe we'd better hold off on this discussion till tomorrow," Sharon suggested gently. "Maybe after a good night's sleep, because actually we're just getting—"

"No, no, no," I lamented. "Let's see it through to the bitter end, the whole hideous truth."

"Daaa-ud!" The voice came from somewhere near my left elbow—urgent, full of frustration, almost tearful.

Peevishly, I glanced down, straight into the face of our three-year-old Shannon. "What, Shannon? Can't you see we're talking about something important?"

"Dad—" She extended her arms. The words were imploring, a bit fearful. "I love ya," she said.

We hugged each other for a long time after that. Long enough for everything to shift and settle—for a proper perspective.

The Rocks

BARBARA B. SMITH

A friend once told me of how he and his wife had allowed a mundane task to be transformed into a regenerative experience that strengthened their relationship:

"My wife and I decided to face the front of our home with rocks. So I called around and located a place where I could get them. I started to get into my truck when my wife called to me and said, 'Let me go with you and help you get the rocks.' I love to have her with me and so I was pleased.

"When we arrived at the place where the rocks were located, we found them on top of a hill. I complained 'What a job! That will be really tough to get all of those rocks down here and loaded into the truck.'

"My wife said, 'You stay here. I'll go up to the top of the hill and roll the rocks down to you. Then, you'll just have to carry them over to the truck. How does that sound?' I thought it was a good idea. I watched her climb to the top of the hill and disappear for a few minutes.

"Soon she called out, 'Look out, dear. Here comes the first one.'

"Then another and another. 'Oh, Bob,' she exclaimed, 'This one has real character.' Then, 'You'll love this one. Here's my favorite. I hope this one isn't too heavy for you to carry.'

"Believe me, I was determined I could carry anything she could roll down. She actually had me anxiously waiting for each rock.

"I enjoyed getting those rocks. I had thought it would be such a job. But, when my bride of over thirty years came down into that meadow that afternoon I fell in love with her all over again. I loved being there where she was surrounded by the beauties of nature. I loved thinking back over the years to the classes she had taken in sculpturing so that she could do busts of our five children. I loved the fact that she had made an intensive study of food and nutrition in order to make us a healthier, happier family. I thought of the many times I sat beside her in church. All of these experiences were ones of interest and joy beyond what I would have known without her. She had expanded my life far beyond what it could have possibly been without her."

How to Prepare a Lesson

KATHLEEN "CASEY" NULL

Although I am about to describe to you the proper methods of lesson preparation by using Relief Society as an example, these methods will also work for a priesthood, Sunday School, or Primary lesson as well. This particular method is geared to parents.

1. Locate lesson manual. If all else fails try the kids' room, toybox, dog house, etc. Remember it's a good idea to keep the lesson manual in a safe place, like on top of the refrigerator or on the uppermost shelves along with three quarters of the household items. Better to be safe than to find your manual cut up for paper dolls.

2. Borrow another lesson manual from auxiliary president.

3. Read lesson.

4. Get the dog out of the crib. Put the baby in the crib. Take the dog food out of the baby's mouth.

5. Finish reading lesson.

6. Start the spaghetti. Answer the phone. Check the batteries in your toddler's barking-wagging dog. Explain to your toddler that the doggie is just tired and needs to take a nap.

7. Make a list of visual and other aids needed.

8. Turn off spaghetti. Clean up mess from where it boiled over. Hurry up and make sauce. Tell your son that if he doesn't collect his socks you will collect them and make a bonfire out of them.

9. Collect materials for visual aids.

10. Make a bottle and tell son to give it to crying baby. Reassure him that you will delay bonfire. Make salad. Answer phone.

11. Spread out poster board. Look for marking pens, scissors, glue, and construction paper. Reassure toddler that he can help you make posters next time.

12. Tell son to get off roof and that if he threw a sock full of dirt up there last summer you don't want it retrieved anyway—ever.

13. Begin to design visual aids with crayons your toddler happily supplied when you couldn't find the marking pens.

14. Serve dinner. Get baby up. Change her clothes. Change her bed. Put her in high chair.

15. Wipe the spaghetti sauce off the lesson manual.

· 16. Send son to hall for a time out for putting peas in his nostrils.

17. Put finished visual aids on high shelf and begin to type handout material.

18. Feed baby. Pick peas from her hair, high chair crevices, and shelves on other side of room.

19. Pick squished pea out of typewriter keys and finish typing.

20. Give baby a bath. Put socks in washing machine. Answer phone. Remember, belatedly, boy on time out. Get dog out of high chair. Remind son to feed dog.

21. White out drawing of the Incredible Hulk that toddler put on handout with, incredibly enough, a marking pen.

22. Put kids to bed. Sigh. Eat dinner and relax knowing that your lesson is ready . . . and in only twenty-two easy steps.

23. Answer phone. "This is Sister Williams reminding you that there will be no lesson this Sunday because of the special Primary program. Hello? . . . Anybody there?"

The Book of Mormon That Wanted to Go First Class

KRIS MACKAY

Landing briefly at Denver, watching many of the other passengers deplane, Anna Packer reached down for her Book of Mormon. She never traveled anywhere without taking it along—and she traveled extensively. Earlier today she had carefully settled the book on top of a box nestled at her feet. Now she had a few quiet moments to savor its familiar passages. She was currently into 3 Nephi and eager to read those inspiring words once again. Her hand touched the box, but not the book. She felt again. She searched around and under her seat. She looked under the feet of remaining passengers nearby. She stood up, peering up and down the aisle, but eventually had to admit that her book was undeniably gone.

Before long the loud-speaking system crackled, and a sweet, feminine voice intoned: "Ladies and gentlemen, a straying Bible has been found. If you can describe it, you may claim it by contacting me in the galley."

Anna moved toward the front of the plane, and between the first row of the tourist section and the beginnings of first class she encountered a stewardess. Anna asked, "Does that Bible happen to be a Book of Mormon? If so, I believe it belongs to me."

The stewardess confirmed that it was a Book of Mormon, asked Anna to wait, and as she disappeared into first class a large, confident-appearing woman in the first row spoke up firmly: "That book *cannot* be yours. It was found in first class."

But the stewardess returned, listened to Anna's explanation

that her missing book was brand spanking new, as this one was, and then placed it into her hands. How did the stewardess come to have it? She explained: "It was the funniest thing! This 'Bible' just came sliding down the aisle into first class—all by itself." Then, with a start, the stewardess realized she had other end-of-flight duties to perform and hurried off down the aisle.

That wasn't the end of the story. After a short conversation with Anna, the woman in the first row asked, "Are you a Mormon?" Anna said, "Yes, I am." The next question was, "Are you a good one?" Anna replied with a smile, "I try to be." The woman said, "Then I'd like to read that book."

Anna didn't hesitate. She gave it away gladly, without a second's thought.

The woman sitting next to the first woman said, "I'd like to read it, too!" Anna doesn't consider herself to be super organized with pencil and paper at the ready, always neatly stored in her purse, but that afternoon they just happened to be there, waiting. Taking the second woman's name and address, she promised to send her a duplicate book the minute she arrived home.

Anna returned to her seat and buckled her seatbelt. The plane would take off soon on the next leg of the flight.

Several hours later they were approaching Atlanta. The busy stewardess sped by, but paused long enough to whisper in Anna's ear, "I was in Salt Lake once, and I was impressed with what I saw. I think I'd like to read that book, too." But before Anna could whip out her pencil, the young woman whizzed off down the aisle, calling over her shoulder that there was no time to write down her address.

Anna was disappointed. Receiving two requests for copies of the book she loved to share was exciting, but three copies not only requested but placed—all on one trip and from most unusual contacts initiated by the book itself—would have been even better. Was it too late? If she wrote a note listing her own address, perhaps she could hand it to the young woman as she left the plane. But there were several stewardesses on board, and two of them resembled each other closely. Anna wasn't sure she could pick out the one who'd shown the interest.

She did write a note as they taxied down the Atlanta runway, just in case, and when the plane reached its dock and the seatbelt sign was extinguished she bounded out of her seat, determined to scurry to the front row, to use that moment before deplaning to try to identify the woman she sought. Her well-laid plan, however, was not to be. A father and daughter were up before she was, and when she politely requested permission to step ahead of them the girl flatly refused. By then the aisles were packed. There was no possibility of anything other than marching off the plane in step.

Anna was near the outside door when a stewardess—the right stewardess, *her* stewardess—ran from first class, clutching a slip of paper in her hand. She called out, "I've got a note for you," to which Anna joyfully replied, "I've got a note for you, too." They exchanged papers—addresses—and when Anna reached Oakland she wasted no time at all in forwarding the two promised books.

Looking back at her travels, this is one of Anna Packer's most cherished memories. Never again has she been approached by three fellow travelers on one trip, asking eagerly for what she was so willing to give.

Secretly Anna suspects it all came about because a particularly strong-minded copy of the Book of Mormon was determined to go first class.

$\mathscr{S}$ources and Permissions

Love

"The Chosen One" by Katherine R. Warner, from Elaine Cannon, *As a Woman Thinketh* (Salt Lake City: Bookcraft, 1990), pp. 80–84.

"In Heaven with You" by Elaine Cannon, from *Love You* (Salt Lake City: Bookcraft, 1991), p. 8.

"Baptism of a Less-Than-Perfect Family" by Marilynne Todd Linford, from *Give Mom a Standing Ovation* (Salt Lake City: Bookcraft, 1996), pp. 66–67.

"Love Did What Anger Never Could" by Sherrie Johnson, from *Spiritually Centered Motherhood* (Salt Lake City: Bookcraft, 1983), pp. 90–91.

"A Mother of Seven" by David O. McKay, from *True to the Faith,* comp. Llewelyn R. McKay (Salt Lake City: Bookcraft, 1966), pp. 174–76.

"Steven Schreyer" by Barbara Timothy Bowen, from Linda J. Eyre, *An Emotional First Aid Kit for Mothers* (Salt Lake City: Bookcraft, 1997), p. 43.

"Rachael" by Anita Canfield, from *A Woman for All Seasons* (Salt Lake City: Bookcraft, 1986), pp. 161–62.

"Love Among Ashes" by Elaine Cannon, from *Love You* (Salt Lake City: Bookcraft, 1991), pp. 26–27.

"A Righteous Prayer" by Brookie Peterson, from *A Woman's Hope* (Salt Lake City: Bookcraft, 1991), p. 82.

"I Like Pwickely Hair" by Barbara Timothy Bowen, from Linda J. Eyre, *An Emotional First Aid Kit for Mothers* (Salt Lake City: Bookcraft, 1997), pp. 46–47.

"A Broken Heart" by Richard M. Siddoway, from *Mom—and Other Great Women I've Known* (Salt Lake City: Bookcraft, 1994), pp. 92–101.

A Woman's Influence

"Trudy Is My Neighbor! My Friend!" by Elaine Cannon, from *Count Your Many Blessings* (Salt Lake City: Bookcraft, 1995), pp. 68–69.

"Sister Barnes" by Barbara B. Smith, from *A Fruitful Season* (Salt Lake City: Bookcraft, 1988), pp. 5–7.

"Becky, a Real MVP" by Marilynne Todd Linford, from *Give Mom a Standing Ovation* (Salt Lake City: Bookcraft, 1996), pp. 147–48.

"The Highest Place of Honor" by David O. McKay, from *True to the Faith,* comp. Llewelyn R. McKay (Salt Lake City: Bookcraft, 1966), p. 284.

"Words" by Ida Isaacson, from Barbara B. Smith and Shirley W. Thomas, *Where Feelings Flower* (Salt Lake City: Bookcraft, 1992), p. 37.

"To My Visiting Teachers" by Emma Lou Thayne, from Barbara B. Smith and Shirley W. Thomas, *Where Feelings Flower* (Salt Lake City: Bookcraft, 1992), p. 94.

"Life: A Precious Gift" by Barbara B. Smith, from *Growth in Grandmothering* (Salt Lake City: Bookcraft, 1986), pp. 4–5.

"A Visiting Teacher Is . . ." by Kathleen "Casey" Null, from *Where Are We Going Besides Crazy?* (Salt Lake City: Bookcraft, 1989), p. 123.

"Far-Reaching Effects" by Anita Canfield, from *A Woman for All Seasons* (Salt Lake City: Bookcraft, 1986), pp. 72–73.

"A Woman's Influence" by David O. McKay, from *True to the Faith,* comp. Llewelyn R. McKay (Salt Lake City: Bookcraft, 1966), pp. 283–84.

Motherhood

"My Kingdom" by Susan Evans McCloud, from *Songs of Life* (Salt Lake City: Bookcraft, 1985), p. 41.

"I've Decided We Need to Start Seeing Other People" by Barbara Timothy Bowen, from Linda J. Eyre, *An Emotional First Aid Kit for Mothers* (Salt Lake City: Bookcraft, 1997), p. 30.

"Exactly How Many Should We Buy?" by Earlene Blaser, from Linda J. Eyre, *An Emotional First Aid Kit for Mothers* (Salt Lake City: Bookcraft, 1997), pp. 82–83.

"101 Acts That Say 'I Love You'" by Marilynne Todd Linford, from *Give Mom a Standing Ovation* (Salt Lake City: Bookcraft, 1996), pp. 155–58.

"Teach Her of Me" by Sherrie Johnson, from *Spiritually Centered Motherhood* (Salt Lake City: Bookcraft, 1983), pp. 1–3.

"Sleep Well" by Barbara Timothy Bowen, from Linda J. Eyre, *An Emotional First Aid Kit for Mothers* (Salt Lake City: Bookcraft, 1997), p. 34.

"First Experience" by Janene Wolsey Baadsgaard, from *On the*

Roller Coaster Called Motherhood (Salt Lake City: Bookcraft, 1990), pp. 3–7. Used by permission.

"A Beginning" by Virginia H. Pearce, from *Connections: Musings About Motherhood* (Salt Lake City: Bookcraft, 1995), pp. 1–4.

"What Would You Do?" by Kathleen "Casey" Null, from *Where Are We Going Besides Crazy?* (Salt Lake City: Bookcraft, 1989), p. 51.

"The Red Shoes" by Mabel Gabbott, from *Mothers in Miniature* (Salt Lake City: Bookcraft, 1976), pp. 16–19.

"Mother, Was It I?" by Brookie Peterson, from *A Woman's Hope* (Salt Lake City: Bookcraft, 1991), pp. 54–55.

Service and Compassion

"Gentlemen of Mercy" by Elaine Cannon, from *Count Your Many Blessings* (Salt Lake City: Bookcraft, 1995), pp. 24–26.

"Learning to Receive" by Ann W. Orton, from Linda J. Eyre, *An Emotional First Aid Kit for Mothers* (Salt Lake City: Bookcraft, 1997), pp. 124–26.

"The Pahoran Principle" by Marilynne Todd Linford, from *Give Mom a Standing Ovation* (Salt Lake City: Bookcraft, 1996), pp. 40–42.

"Service Becomes Less of a Sacrifice" by Michaelene Grassli, from *LeaderTalk* (Salt Lake City: Bookcraft, 1996), pp. 13–14.

"Just Make Him Stop," Name Withheld, from Sharon Clonts and Janice Chalker, *From Pain to Peace* (Salt Lake City: Bookcraft, 1993), p. 89.

"One Winter's Night" by David O. McKay, from *True to the Faith,* comp. Llewelyn R. McKay (Salt Lake City: Bookcraft, 1966), pp. 166–67.

"The Day We Picked the Beans" by Mabel Gabbott, from *Mothers in Miniature* (Salt Lake City: Bookcraft, 1976), pp. 12–13.

" 'Silver and Gold Have I None; But Such As I Have Give I Thee'" by H. Burke Peterson, from *A Glimpse of Glory* (Salt Lake City: Bookcraft, 1986), pp. 93–96.

"Statistics of Service" by Marilynne Todd Linford, from *Give Mom a Standing Ovation* (Salt Lake City: Bookcraft, 1996), pp. 9–10.

"Sister Anderson" by Barbara B. Smith, from *A Fruitful Season* (Salt Lake City: Bookcraft, 1988), pp. 25–27.

"Let's Do Your Hair" by Elaine Cannon, from *As a Woman Thinketh* (Salt Lake City: Bookcraft, 1990), p. 134.

Faith and Hope

"Let Your Hearts Be Comforted" by Kris Mackay, from *Gift of Love* (Salt Lake City: Bookcraft, 1990), pp. 39–42.

"Answered Prayer" by Susan Evans McCloud, from *Songs of Life* (Salt Lake City: Bookcraft, 1985), p. 58.

"Returning Good for Evil" by Elaine Cannon, from *Count Your Many Blessings* (Salt Lake City: Bookcraft, 1995), pp. 94–96.

"I Will Wait for Spring" by Janene Wolsey Baadsgaard, from *On the Roller Coaster Called Motherhood* (Salt Lake City: Bookcraft, 1990), pp. 76–78. Used by permission.

"Bill," Name Withheld, from Sharon Clonts and Janice Chalker,

From Pain to Peace (Salt Lake City: Bookcraft, 1993), pp. 30–31.

"Coins" by Jean Chapin Seifert, from Barbara B. Smith and Shirley W. Thomas, *Where Feelings Flower* (Salt Lake City: Bookcraft, 1992), p. 57.

"The Mountain That Moved (Almost)" by Kris Mackay, from *The Outstretched Arms* (Salt Lake City: Bookcraft, 1983), pp. 67–72.

"A Lesson in Faith" by Elaine Cannon, from *Count Your Many Blessings* (Salt Lake City: Bookcraft, 1995), pp. 100–102.

"Mary Fielding Smith and the Journey West" by Garrett H. Garff. Previously unpublished.

"Thy Ways" by Susan Evans McCloud, from *Songs of Life* (Salt Lake City: Bookcraft, 1985), p. 22.

Marriage and Family

"The Panty Hose Problem" by Elaine Cannon, from *Love You* (Salt Lake City: Bookcraft, 1991), pp. 82–83.

"A Son Brings His Family into the Church" by Barbara B. Smith, from *A Fruitful Season* (Salt Lake City: Bookcraft, 1988), pp. 92–93.

"For Lack of Love and Attention" by Janene Wolsey Baadsgaard, from *On the Roller Coaster Called Motherhood* (Salt Lake City: Bookcraft, 1990), pp. 16–17. Used by permission.

"Large Family" by Kathleen "Casey" Null, from *Where Are We Going Besides Crazy?* (Salt Lake City: Bookcraft, 1989), p. 38.

"Another Baby?" by Linda J. Eyre, from *A Joyful Mother of Children* (Salt Lake City: Bookcraft, 1983), pp. 14–19.

"Family Home Evenings in Your Little House" by George Durrant, from *You and Your Spouse in Your Happy House* (Salt Lake City: Bookcraft, 1992), pp. 65–67.

"I'll Bet You Don't Know What Day This Is" by Brookie Peterson, from *A Woman's Hope* (Salt Lake City: Bookcraft, 1991), p. 29.

"Boys" by Kathleen "Casey" Null, from *Where Are We Going Besides Crazy?* (Salt Lake City: Bookcraft, 1989), pp. 42–43.

"The Little Rescuer" by Elaine L. Jack, from " 'Never Take No Cut-offs' or 'You Have Nothing to Fear from the Journey,'" *1993–94 Devotional and Fireside Speeches* (Provo, UT: Brigham Young University Press, 1994), p. 42.

"Kidding Around in Your Little House" by George Durrant, from *You and Your Spouse in Your Happy House* (Salt Lake City: Bookcraft, 1992), pp. 95–99.

"What Can I Be?" by Patricia T. Holland, from "Filling the Measure of Your Creation," *1988–89 Devotional and Fireside Speeches* (Provo, UT: Brigham Young University Press, 1989), p. 71.

Seeking the Spirit

"Taking Down Fences" by Ardeth G. Kapp, from *Echoes from My Prairie* (Salt Lake City: Bookcraft, 1979), pp. 17–22.

"Mom, We Need to Talk" by Earlene Blaser, from Linda J. Eyre, *An Emotional First Aid Kit for Mothers* (Salt Lake City: Bookcraft, 1997), pp. 63–64.

"It's My Baby!" by Barbara B. Smith, from *A Fruitful Season* (Salt Lake City: Bookcraft, 1988), pp. 28-30.

"The White Handkerchief" by Marilynne Todd Linford, from *Give*

Mom a Standing Ovation (Salt Lake City: Bookcraft, 1996), pp. 14–15.

"All Prayers Are Answered" by Sherrie Johnson, from *Spiritually Centered Motherhood* (Salt Lake City: Bookcraft, 1983), pp. 34–35.

"End of Rope" by Kathleen "Casey" Null, from *Where Are We Going Besides Crazy?* (Salt Lake City: Bookcraft, 1989), pp. 41–42.

"Nourish Both Physically and Spiritually" by Barbara B. Smith, from *The Love That Never Faileth* (Salt Lake City: Bookcraft, 1984), pp. 130–31.

"One of My Worst Weaknesses" by Anita Canfield, from *A Woman for All Seasons* (Salt Lake City: Bookcraft, 1986), pp. 89–90.

"A Preference for Primary" by Camille Fronk, from "Lessons from the Potter and the Clay" *1994–95 Devotional and Fireside Speeches* (Provo, UT: Brigham Young University Press, 1995), p. 139.

"Strong-Willed Children," Name Withheld, from Sharon Clonts and Janice Chalker, *From Pain to Peace* (Salt Lake City: Bookcraft, 1993), pp. 31–32.

Gratitude and Appreciation

"Discrepancy" by Susan Evans McCloud, from *Songs of Life* (Salt Lake City: Bookcraft, 1985), p. 20.

"I Am Grateful for the Trials I Have Not Had" by Elaine Cannon, from *Count Your Many Blessings* (Salt Lake City: Bookcraft, 1995), pp. 82–83.

"My Life Is Not How I Would Have Written It" by Barbara Timothy Bowen, from Linda J. Eyre, *An Emotional First Aid Kit for*

Mothers (Salt Lake City: Bookcraft, 1997), pp. 14–15.

"Expressions of Appreciation" by Michaelene Grassli, from *LeaderTalk* (Salt Lake City: Bookcraft, 1996), pp. 106–7.

"Contrasts" by Helen M. Terry, from Barbara B. Smith and Shirley W. Thomas, *Where Feelings Flower* (Salt Lake City: Bookcraft, 1992), p. 35.

"Gratitude" by Albert L. Zobell, Jr., from *Story Beacons* (Salt Lake City: Bookcraft, 1957), pp. 34–35.

"The Hammer" by Marilynne Todd Linford, from *Give Mom a Standing Ovation* (Salt Lake City: Bookcraft, 1996), p. 96.

"To a Mother-in-Law in Israel" by Alice Brady Myers, from Barbara B. Smith and Shirley W. Thomas, *Where Feelings Flower* (Salt Lake City: Bookcraft, 1992), p. 75.

Finding Peace and Balance in Life

"You're the Princess" by Barbara Timothy Bowen, from Linda J. Eyre, *An Emotional First Aid Kit for Mothers* (Salt Lake City: Bookcraft, 1997), pp. 43–44.

"Thanks, Jacob, I Needed That" by Janene Wolsey Baadsgaard, from *On the Roller Coaster Called Motherhood* (Salt Lake City: Bookcraft, 1990), pp. 28–30. Used by permission.

"For Example" by Kathryn Kay, from Barbara B. Smith and Shirley W. Thomas, *Where Feelings Flower* (Salt Lake City: Bookcraft, 1992), p. 28.

"Lovely, Lonely Home" by Kathleen "Casey" Null, from *Where Are We Going Besides Crazy?* (Salt Lake City: Bookcraft, 1989), pp. 4–5.

"Bob and Weave" by Elaine L. Jack, from "Them and Us" *1990–91 Devotional and Fireside Speeches* (Provo, UT: Brigham Young University Press, 1991), pp. 131–32.

"My Particular Love Is Music" by Linda J. Eyre, from *A Joyful Mother of Children* (Salt Lake City: Bookcraft, 1983), pp. 76–78.

"Kindness" by Marilynne Todd Linford, from *A Woman Fulfilled* (Salt Lake City: Bookcraft, 1992), pp. 38–39.

"Thanksgiving Treasure" by Janene Wolsey Baadsgaard, from *On the Roller Coaster Called Motherhood* (Salt Lake City: Bookcraft, 1990), pp. 41–43. Used by permission.

"Sunday Incident" by Anita Canfield, from *A Woman for All Seasons* (Salt Lake City: Bookcraft, 1986), pp. 111–15.

"Things That Ease the Strain" by Emma Lou Thayne, from *As for Me and My House* (Salt Lake City: Bookcraft, 1989), pp. 69–71.

Finding Joy and Humor in Life

"Find Joy in the Service of God" by Michaelene Grassli, from *LeaderTalk* (Salt Lake City: Bookcraft, 1996), pp. 125–27.

"The Bitter and the Sweet" by Janene Wolsey Baadsgaard, from *On the Roller Coaster Called Motherhood* (Salt Lake City: Bookcraft, 1990), pp. 74–76. Used by permission.

"I Just Don't Think It's Worth It" by Earlene Blaser, from Linda J. Eyre, *An Emotional First Aid Kit for Mothers* (Salt Lake City: Bookcraft, 1997), p. 90.

"A Matter of Attitude" by Brookie Peterson, from *A Woman's Hope* (Salt Lake City: Bookcraft, 1991), pp. 7–8.

"Bat Man" by Karen J. Ashton, from *Behold Your Little Ones* (Salt Lake City: Bookcraft, 1999), p. 65.

"A Proper Perspective" by Gordon T. Allred, from *My Home Runneth Over* (Salt Lake City: Bookcraft, 1980), pp. 17–19.

"The Rocks" by Barbara B. Smith, from *The Love That Never Faileth* (Salt Lake City: Bookcraft, 1984), pp. 111–12.

"How to Prepare a Lesson" by Kathleen "Casey" Null, from *Where Are We Going Besides Crazy?* (Salt Lake City: Bookcraft, 1989), pp. 116–18.

"The Book of Mormon That Wanted to Go First Class" by Kris Mackay, from *The Ultimate Love* (Salt Lake City: Bookcraft, 1994), pp. 92–94.

In the works are plans to publish additional volumes in the *Sunshine for the Latter-day Saint Soul* series. Bookcraft invites readers to contribute to the collection of literature from which stories for subsequent volumes will be selected.

Stories may be up to 1,500 words in length and must reflect Latter-day Saint values and principles, as well as uplift and inspire readers. If you have such a story, take the time to write it down. Likewise, encourage others who may have uplifting stories to write them down and submit them. All stories will be subject to editorial review.

Send your stories to:

Sunshine for the Latter-day Saint Soul
2405 West Orton Circle
West Valley City, UT 84119
Fax: 801-908-3401
E-mail: sunshine@ldsworld.com

Please include your name, address, and a daytime phone number with all submissions.